Willed in His Grace

Willed in His Grace

*One Woman's Journey
from Poverty to Spiritual Wealth*

Laura Jaka

MOUNTAIN ARBOR
PRESS
Alpharetta, GA

The author has tried to recreate events, locations, and conversations from her memories of them. In some instances, in order to maintain their anonymity, the author has changed the names of individuals and places. She may also have changed some identifying characteristics and details such as physical attributes, occupations, and places of residence.

Copyright © 2019 by Laura Jaka

All rights reserved. No part of this book may be reproduced or transmitted in any form or by any means, electronic or mechanical, including photocopying, recording, or any information storage and retrieval system, without permission in writing from the author.

ISBN: 978-1-63183-613-8 - Paperback
ISBN: 978-1-63183-614-5 - ePub
eISBN: 978-1-63183-615-2 - Mobi

Library of Congress Control Number: 2019912035

Printed in the United States of America   082719

∞This paper meets the requirements of ANSI/NISO Z39.48-1992 (Permanence of Paper)

Scripture quotations marked "CSB" are from the Christian Standard Bible, copyright © 2017 by Holman Bible Publishers. Used by permission. Christian Standard Bible® and CSB® are federally registered trademarks of Holman Bible Publishers, all rights reserved.
Scripture quotations marked "ESV" are from the ESV® Bible (The Holy Bible, English Standard Version®), copyright © 2001 by Crossway, a publishing ministry of Good News Publishers. Used by permission. All rights reserved.
Scriptures marked as "GNT" are taken from the Good News Translation, Second Edition © 1992 by American Bible Society. Used by permission.
Scripture quotations marked "KJV" are taken from the Holy Bible, King James Version (Public Domain).
Scripture quotations marked "NIV" are taken from the Holy Bible, New International Version®, NIV®. Copyright © 1973, 1978, 1984 by Biblica, Inc.™ Used by permission of Zondervan. All rights reserved worldwide.

To my grandmother, my "Mamma," whom God allowed to breathe life in me for the first thirteen years of my life.

You taught me that I am most valuable to others when I am incomplete. You showed me that poverty should not be an excuse that prevents me from adhering to my calling. Instead, the spirit of tenacity should serve as my moral compass in all I dare to undertake. You taught me that I don't have to be rich in order to serve in any capacity where there's a need. I learned firsthand from you the meaning of sacrifice. Most importantly, you taught me that compassion should be at the forefront of all my relationships. All of your teachings will forever be engraved in my heart.

I am forever indebted to you, Mamma, for all of your sacrifices.

And all these blessings shall come on thee, and overtake thee, if thou shalt hearken unto the voice of the LORD thy God.

—Deuteronomy 28:2 (KJV)

Contents

Preface	xi
Acknowledgments	xiii
Introduction	xv
Chapter One: Was It 1976 or 1977?	1
Chapter Two: Family	3
Chapter Three: Coming to America	33
Chapter Four: Georgia	61
Chapter Five: Thou Art My God!	81
Chapter Six: "Your Word, O Lord, Is Truth; Consecrate Us in the Truth"	91
Chapter Seven: Forever Desperate for My Heavenly Father's Touch	101
Chapter Eight: Dearest Camilla	105
Chapter Nine: Dear Future Husband	115
Chapter Ten: Appeal to Love	121

Preface

It's surreal that I have gotten an opportunity to write a book in which I pay homage to the woman who sacrificed everything to raise my siblings and me, offer a few of the fantastic stories about God and me, unveil myself to my daughter by sharing details of my life that I had not previously shared, and express what love means to me and what I desire in my future husband.

I would never have fathomed this to be my story. Although I had written a couple of pieces while dealing with a heartbreak, and another inspired by a client, and yet another by my mother, I didn't think that on the fourteenth anniversary of my beloved grandmother's death on September 28, 2018, when I decided to write a short piece in honor of her, that I would be inspired to write the rest of this book.

I have experienced challenging times in my life and have navigated some treacherous territories. Nevertheless, all has come full circle, as I have managed to utilize those experiences to my advantage. It's true that I have not mastered it all, but I have overcome a lot. To think that I am the only one in my entire family thus far to have attained a college education is one achievement that I count as a tremendous blessing. Now, owning my own business, working in the same field for over two decades, doing what I love, and having the opportunity to serve others are nothing short of proof of God's unwavering love toward me.

I feel tremendously blessed. I am grateful to God for all that He continues to do in my life.

I am exceptionally grateful to God for my daughter. Being responsible for another human life is extremely scary, but also rewarding at the same time. I could not have been the woman that I am today if God hadn't chosen me to foster one of His own. She inspires me daily and serves as my moral compass. She's secretly the key that has unlocked many of my values.

I am grateful that my mother and I developed a relationship, and that we have continued to learn about each other. I treasure the way my brothers have evolved and have come into their own. Also, I am an aunt to two beautiful nieces and a nephew whose love and affection I treasure with every bit of me.

I've come to a place in my life where very few things ruffle my feathers. My life's journey thus far has ushered me into a place of completeness. What do I mean by that? I have learned to be still in those moments where I would have otherwise drowned trying to figure everything out. I have come to know that in the end, all things work together for my good (Romans 8:28), and so, I've been positioned in a place of rest as I allow for everything else to fall into place, as it should.

My journey has taught me that in the end, all that matters is love and family.

Having suffered many trials and tribulations, and not evolving into my own until I became a mother are things I consider to have been strategically purposed for me, because nothing happens outside the realms of God's timing. There's nothing about my past of which I am ashamed. I have bottled up the lessons learned throughout my life, and they are the other part of me that has formed the woman I am today.

Acknowledgments

I would like first to thank God for His endless faith in me. Without His infinite grace and mercy, I would not be where I am today. His gift of unconditional love allows me to continue to live my life as beautifully as I am while endeavoring in His confidence.

To my mother, thank you for allowing God to use you to bring me into this world. The odds were stacked up against you. Nevertheless, you thought I was worthy enough for you to continue to endure the scrutiny of our Krio family. I am grateful for your sacrifice.

I am immensely grateful to my daughter, Camilla, for being my point of reference, empowering me daily to dare to be different. You are the best gift that I was unprepared for, but you have filled my life with hope and determination. You help to channel the rest of what I am becoming.

To all of my clients and their families, colleagues, and staff members, you have been a valuable instrument for God to teach me the virtue of prudence. Your expectations of me, although at times challenging, help to shape my overall being. You play a pivotal role in my life that many of you are not aware of. For that, I am grateful. Thank you for trusting me to lead in the capacity that I have the privilege to serve.

To my entire family, we have had a very long journey. I am so thankful to God that He has afforded us the opportunity to find ourselves. We have withstood many challenges, but God has positioned Himself on our behalf. We have all that we need to continue to endeavor: God. Thank you, every one of you, for your trust and continued support of me. I am thankful that God placed me in the midst of you.

To the handful of friends that have inspired me to be better, some of you were (and others continue to be) an oasis that God placed in my life to allow me to mature. The rest of you have taught me patience, resilience, and tenacity. You force me to challenge myself to overcome those areas of my life in which I would otherwise feel timid. I treasure your friendships. Thank you for your continued dedication.

To my support system in Africa, Europe, Wisconsin, and Georgia, my and Camilla's lives are what they are because you allowed God to selflessly use you to shepherd us in our times of need. Your dedication and support are gifts that we'll always treasure in our hearts. You will forever be a part of our lives. We thank you from the bottom of our hearts.

Introduction

This book began with a tribute to my grandmother, "Mamma." I never knew this book would become what it turned out to be. In it, I've had the privilege to share the blessings that my Mamma passed on to my siblings and me. I share how her tenacity, resilience, compassion, sacrifice, and love transformed my life.

I also had the opportunity to share the many storms I have weathered, and how I have been able to accomplish all of my assignments thus far, which is only by the grace of God.

This journey has been therapeutic for me, as it has allowed me to open up and share the difficulties associated with my assignments, and how God has triumphantly used me in the process. I've come to realize that everything God does serves a purpose.

As a child, I learned firsthand from my grandmother how vital it is to be generous. I learned that I do not have to be a rich person in order to give to others who are in need. I learned the essence of compassion, which is a trait that my beloved grandmother bestowed upon me.

I have now come to know that the birth of this book was no coincidence, but rather purposeful. It was predestined, as I wholeheartedly believe that I, too, am now in the position of what my grandmother was to my siblings and me, and to our community in Sierra Leone. My grandmother obeyed her calling to serve when she was in the most disadvantageous position of her life. She was inspired to be a steward to many, even though she had absolutely nothing to give. Although Mamma was financially deprived, she was gracefully obedient to her calling with the very little she had.

It was in August of 2017 when I learned of the mudslide that killed hundreds of people in my birth country of Sierra Leone. On August 14, 2017, as CNN broadcast the news of the mudslide that left hundreds dead and many more homeless, I sat on my bed with tears streaming down my face, asking for God to use me on their behalf. I was broken and hurt at the same time.

Moved with passion, I immediately wrote a brief write-up about the incident and opened a donation page on Facebook and GoFundMe. I shared the links with everyone I knew and asked for their support. Few people donated, many prayed, while others simply dismissed my request. However, I was grateful for it all.

In September of 2018, I visited the middle-of-nowhere, dirt-filled environment where the victims now lived, an area called Mile 6. While visiting, I learned that there had also been another flood that had killed many more and left the surviving victims in deplorable living conditions. I took what was donated and also gave what I was able to donate. Since then, I have continued in my quest to help those in need by contributing financially to their needs. My quest to bring awareness and support to these victims has only heightened.

During my visit, we prayed, danced, and cried together. They were grateful. I felt like I belonged there. In fact, I knew that I belonged there. It was natural for me to be in the midst of them. Right then and there, I thought to myself that perhaps I had been called into a royal position for such a time as this (Esther 4:14, NIV).

It was in August of 2017 when I asked God to use me to help and bring awareness to these victims in hopes of a better outcome. A year later, He afforded me the opportunity to meet the people for whom I had prayed. And, when I was writing this book—which took me about five weeks to complete—that still small voice inside of me stirred the desire for me to donate the proceeds of the sale of this book to their cause.

Without hesitation, I obliged.

Before my visit last year to Mile 6, I had a dream that I was being led by three people—two people in the front and one in the back—to an unfamiliar place similar to a farm with a small pan-body house.

A pan-body house is one of the few traditional homes in Sierra Leone. The construction of these homes is from zinc, which has no insulation or flooring. These makeshift homes sit above the bare ground and are scattered all around the country, as some of the most impoverished individuals use them. A pan-body house lacks the necessities required for an ideal home.

In the dream, I stood in the middle of these people, walking straight ahead. As we walked, I saw an empty field full of green grass. Its entire circumference was green. There was a small bridge that we had to cross over to get to the other side. There was a small, unkempt bed right in the middle of the bridge. The sheet on the bed was blue with some residue on it. Also on the bridge was a black wheelchair.

I would have to climb over the bed to get to the other side of the bridge. Ordinarily, I would think the bed unclean and the location unsafe. However, without thinking it through, I climbed over the bed and crossed to the other side.

The people in front of me walked into the pan-body house. Immediately, I began to share with them that someone had passed away in the house. In this moment, I woke from the dream.

The miraculous thing about all of this is that the place in my dream was exactly how the campsite looked when I visited. Amazingly, this was my first visit to this location. Interestingly, we had to stop on two separate occasions to get directions (I went with two of my brothers). When we stopped for the first time, we asked a couple of men by the roadside for directions to Mile 6. As we got closer to the location, we again stopped and met a girl who lived at one of the campsites. She shared that she was returning home from running errands. She instructed us on how to get to Mile 6, but also led us by walking ahead as we drove behind her.

None of these events are coincidences. I have experienced God speaking in subtle ways firsthand, so I recognize this calling with all certainty. Therefore, I have pledged that a substantial amount of the proceeds from the sale of this book will be donated to Mile 6 to help improve the victims' overall current living conditions.

Chapter One

Was It 1976 or 1977?

Was I born in 1976 or 1977? This question has been a debate between my mother and me. She believes I was born on February 2, 1977. However, my birth certificate, which she signed, reads February 2, 1976. Thus, I have elected to have been born on February 2, 1976.

As I sit here in the space that I have dedicated to Wellington Place of Serenity, my private home-care agency that I will talk more about in another chapter, I find myself gazing around the room. Trust me, there's not much to look at, as it is full of mandatory licensures, documents, and posters. Yet as I sit here, I can't help but think of how my life has measured up to where I am in this present moment, time, and space.

In the past, I would often ask God, "Who am I that you've come to love me this much? What are my duties? Why have you given me so many opportunities and chances throughout my forty-plus years on this earth?" But in the midst of asking Him all of these questions, that sweet, quiet voice inside of me would always say, "It's simple, my darling. I chose you; you did not choose me."

Phenomenal!

In my forty-three years, I will be bold enough to say that I have seen and experienced more than most people in my age group. Therefore, I would boast that these experiences—the trials, tribulations, obstacles, miracles, favors, and triumphs (and the lack thereof)—have all helped shaped the woman that I am today.

Have I mastered it all? Of course not. Do I take credit for those things in which I have excelled? God forbid that I dare think of myself as the key reason for it all. Will I continue to divert from the roads that have been paved for me? Most certainly, I will. Even then, what I am sure of is that through the diversions, God will still direct my path.

In this next chapter, I will share the experiences about the girl who elected to be born on February 2, 1976, versus February 2, 1977, and how God has helped carry her through it all. I believe that this chapter will be a fascinating read for you, as I uncover the roads that I have traveled and the successes gained.

Do you realize I said "successes"? Yes, successes. All of these roads have led to where I am today.

Chapter Two

Family

Train up a child in the way he should go: and when he is old, he will not depart from it.

—Proverbs 22:6 (KJV)

I elected to be born on February 2, 1976, versus February 2, 1977, contrary to what my mother has held fast to all these years. I must say that there haven't been any further contradictions about my birth year, except when Adju—the name we call my mother—calls to wish me happy birthday yearly. Yes, we argue about it, and then we agree to disagree, but the fact remains that I am a 1976 baby per my decision.

Growing up in Freetown, Sierra Leone, was both advantageous and disadvantageous to my overall development. Little did I know, however, that all of what I considered to be disadvantageous events were circumstances that no other environment could have offered me. I loved my childhood, undoubtedly because a phenomenal woman raised me: my beloved grandmother, Daisy Susanna Wellington, whom we called Mamma.

Mamma and her family were from Congo. She, too, established her nuclear family in Congo before moving to Freetown, Sierra Leone, in 1961. Mamma was able to transition well, but never lost her thick Congolese accent.

Mamma was a fantastic mother and wife. As a child, I watched Mamma serve her children and her husband with love, compassion, dignity, and honor. She loved as only she could. Out of everyone I have come to know, her qualities were unmatched. She saw the good in everyone and never cared to distinguish between upper and middle class. As a child, I admired everything she did, and desired to be like her. Well, God granted my desire.

Mamma raised my siblings and me for most of our childhoods, because my mother was a teenager with no parental experience. Mamma assumed this role without reservation, and she did an exceptional job.

Mamma was one in a million! She was our MVP! My siblings and I loved and adored everything about her. It was a bitter blow to my family when she died in September of 2004. She was seventy-seven years of age. We mourned her, but we were thankful for the years we had with her. She was the matriarch of our family. She was little in stature, but fierce in everything she dared to undertake.

She knew the meaning of sacrifice; she was the very definition of the word. She had very little—poor with absolutely nothing accumulated regarding monetary worth—but she was full of unconditional love. She gave selflessly to us and anyone else who needed the little she had. She never turned anyone away. Even in times that she could not afford to help, she found a way. She was compassionate. She valued family, so she lived by example in an effort that others would model after her. She lowered her wings so many could climb on and soar, and boy, did we fly.

Although there were many occasions when Mamma could have said that we disappointed her, I am sure there were also countless moments of pride and joy that she could boast of in our regard. I learned from her. I modeled myself after her while growing up until the age of about fourteen, when my life changed drastically.

Up until then, I was worth very little to those relatives whom my grandmother had entrusted me with in the hopes that they would nurture and care for me, as she couldn't financially provide for all of my siblings and me. She had all the love in the world, but lacked the money to ensure our overall well-being. She endeavored and sacrificed by putting me up on a couple of occasions with family, one of whom was her eldest son, Sonny, and his nuclear family. The other became a relative through marriage via my maternal grandfather. None of these living arrangements worked out for various reasons.

According to these family members, I was destined for failure and so was my older brother, Richmond. My brother and I, according to them, were no-good children who would never amount to anything. We were labeled, talked about, pointed at, dismissed at every opportunity, and just downright regarded as nothing. These were families with children the same age as my brother and me, or maybe just a few years apart.

Well, to be clear, they couldn't have had compassion as parents toward us, because of the entire family (my grandmother's side, that is), my family was the poorest of them all. We were the ones in need of their handouts and leftovers. We were the maids and cooks for their families.

My grandmother, recognizing our dependence on our relatives, was instrumental in ensuring that we remained humble, because we needed their food and at times their financial assistance to make ends meet. I am by no means suggesting that my brother and I were model children, because we did exhibit the same behaviors as many other children did and still do, but nothing we did as children warranted the actions and treatment we endured by our close relatives who were supposed to have been our mentors.

They were downright mean and nasty, mainly because they did not want to be bothered with us but felt they had to. Uncle was Mamma's son, and Aunty was my grandaunt's sister, so you see, they felt compelled to care for us, but failed to deliver. Instead, they left us wondering why they treated us the way they did and with plenty of insecurities to mend.

The truth is, I don't believe they thought they were doing anything wrong, as their mentality was one of their tribe, in which they were accustomed to a sophisticated way of living. In fact, if you could not meet their "rich standards," then you were an outcast. My cousin calls this "Creoledom." Creoledom was something my family was the subject of almost daily. Of course, Mamma couldn't have cared less, as her primary goal was to feed us and to survive, and these families were our support. Thus, she brushed it off and kept her head held high.

My real mother, Adju, was never around much, and so she endured very little, from what I can remember. Nevertheless, this did not shield her from the Creoledom way of thinking. She was the subject of many false assumptions, including about her intellect. She became a teenage mother when she had her first child at the age of seventeen. By then, she was already the mockery of the family that was full of girls who attended prestigious schools, had personal drivers, maids, and all the privileges in the world. My mother, on the other hand, was not wealthy, and her mother and stepfather could not afford to provide her with such a lifestyle. I don't remember my mother ever associating with any of these people. It was almost as if she, too, felt some rejection from them. Alternatively, perhaps, she knew what they thought of her and graciously kept her distance.

My mother also shares some similarities with my grandmother. She is humble, loving, and compassionate toward others. My mother has the quality of inclusiveness, which I genuinely admire. Even so, she knows when to take a step back and not be bothered with anyone or anything that is not of substance to her in those instances where she feels unappreciated. I am a lot like her in this regard, which is how she treated the Krio side of her family—a justified action, in my opinion.

Ultimately, Adju became a mother of nine. With my grandmother's assistance, she journeyed her course as best as she could. She had her ups and downs, and failed on many occasions, but I have said many times that she's a better mother than I could ever imagine becoming, mainly because she consciously gave birth to all of the children that God entrusted in her care. She's relentless and resilient in her pursuit of being herself, contrary to what the world thinks.

My mother marches to the beat of her own drum and dances to her music. When the time came to decide, she knew that her level of maturity to be a fantastic mother was not fully developed, as she was still a child herself. Recognizing her limitations, she graciously gave her mother the opportunity to raise almost all of her children—an action I never understood as a child, by the way. I thought she was selfish and lazy, and so I did not develop a bond with her. Instead, I regarded my grandmother as my mother, which was a gross misjudgment on my part.

Nonetheless, I thank God that my mother and I have now been able to develop our relationship and are bonding as a mother and daughter should. Of all of my siblings, I resemble my mother the most. While two of my brothers have some of her features, I am the exact image of her. I haven't formed any conclusion regarding our personalities thus far, as I am still getting to know her, except that I am shy, and so is she. She's soft-spoken, and talks to me with such respect that I sense it stems out of guilt. I occasionally point out that I am the child and she, the mother. She does not exemplify the same level of humility toward my brothers, maybe because she has had an opportunity to get to know them better and has been with them for most of their lives. Who knows?

I try to learn more about all of my siblings and my mother when I visit home, but I come up short most of the time, mainly because I don't fully know everyone very well. One thing that puzzled me recently during what was a massive loss for our family was the level of compassion and care I felt for my mother and brothers while I was home. I now have a total of nine brothers (six from my mother and three from my father). I am the only girl, as we lost my baby sister a while back during a tribal war in my country.

During this visit, I gained a level of empathy, one that I had never had before, toward my siblings, because I felt abandoned for the most part since I left home in pursuit of a better life, which was not my decision. I had also become the provider for everyone, just like my grandmother was. I resented that I had to care for everyone at such a young age, and nothing thus far had materialized from my efforts and years of giving.

However, I was wrong. I saw then how unique they are. Although regarded as nothing by many of our Creoledom folks, they demonstrate character—the character and the kind of attitude that would have made my grandmother proud. My assumptions of them had been wrong, as they were striving to the best of their abilities.

They have come to form a sense of self and have developed into their own. Nothing but pride filled my heart upon seeing this. The same goes for my mother, although she did not verbally say it. She had all of her flock in one basket, and we could see the pride and joy in her eyes. At that moment, I believe she thought to herself, *I am still standing in spite of it all.* She must have felt, *My children are still standing, and I am proud of them all.* We are blessed to call her our mother.

I was also amazed at the unity that exists between my brothers. Growing up, we fought, because everyone was headstrong. I thought for sure these guys would have been at each other's throats and so on. Don't get me wrong, they do butt heads, but maturity has set in at its fullest in their regard, and love has manifested itself in my entire family. To God be the glory!

A couple of my brothers are now parents themselves. I adore my little firecracker nieces and mischievous nephew. Their little hearts are full of love and compassion. They all are so perfect, but uniquely diverse. One could not deny the Wellington, Willoughby, Stevens, and the Smith genes that are at play. As I watch them play, fight, or merely be children, I often think of my childhood, except my childhood was very different from theirs. I did not have the privilege to play as much as they do or to bond as they are, because I was too busy being a parent to my younger siblings and a helper to my Mamma.

Like my grandmother, I, too, was responsible for assuming the role of a mother to my mother's children, which was a responsibility I had no idea how to navigate except through imitating Mamma. I can clearly remember how frustrated I would become at times, because I was a child myself, and having to assume such an essential role left me on many occasions very angry. I remember a couple of instances when I was so mean to my little sister and brother because I felt they demanded too much of me. I had no life of my own, so it seemed. I was so embedded in my role as my Mamma's helper and a nurturer to my younger siblings that I could not even focus academically. I had very little time to be a child or student.

Nevertheless, I had a wonderful uncle who ensured I felt relevant. He was my mother's younger brother, Kofi. He and I were inseparable. He took me almost everywhere he went, and at times to places I had no business being, but that's how much he loved me. I knew every place he worked and would visit with him often, because I knew that at the end of his workday, he would buy me something special to eat, which was my treat. He introduced me to all of his girlfriends. Yes, he had several at a time, some of whom thought I was his daughter. He loved me, and he doted on me. Uncle Kofi was humble and kind.

He was like Mamma: he stepped into the shadow and nurtured us to the best of his ability. Uncle Kofi was a young man trying to figure out life, but that didn't stop him from being his mother's son. He demonstrated to us what his mother had passed on to him: unconditional love.

We lost Uncle Kofi very early on during the tribal war in my country, as he had become a soldier. He was a go-getter, very intelligent, and smart. His penmanship was unbelievable. He wrote so nicely that I would be eager to admire everything he wrote. Yes, I loved marveling at his writing, because that was all I could do. I could not read.

During my last visit home, I was surprised that my mother still has some of the love letters Uncle Kofi had written to his girlfriends. In them, his genuineness and zest for life were evident to see. His beautiful handwriting was still visible after all these years. All of us will forever miss him.

I mentioned that we were poor. Well, I don't think I have the right words to stress *how* poor we were. We lived in a one-bedroom flat that barely had room for all of us. Our bathroom was outside, which required us to use the restroom in a bucket at night. Poor Mamma—she was commissioned to follow any of us that needed to go "number two" in the middle of the night with the only lamp we had. She would wait outside the bathroom to ensure our safety.

My siblings and I slept on the floor while Mamma and Uncle Kofi took the bed. We had a few things here and there, which allowed us to call this place home. Things were so bad at times that I would have to breastfeed my younger brother, who cried so horribly due to hunger. Yes, my breasts were undeveloped at the time, but I believed perhaps that the sensation of having a nipple in his mouth would calm him down. My baby brother latched on so tightly that one would conclude that I had breast milk flowing through my bare chest.

This coping mechanism went on for what seemed like forever. While mothering my baby brother, I also served as a role model for my baby sister, who in my opinion was very needy. The girl wanted all the attention in the world. I could at times see how drained Mamma was with having to give herself to all of us. She had no one to lean on concerning moral support. But being who she was, Mamma never complained. Yes, she was a phenomenal woman!

I attended a primary school that was far away from home, while my other sibling of school age attended one near our house. It was a routine for me to walk him to school and continue to my school that was further away. I walked to school barefooted almost always, because I didn't have shoes. My baby brother had the same predicament as me.

Also, I would wear my Mamma's underwear and tie it on each

side because it was too big for me. I didn't have many clothes of my own, so wearing Mamma's underwear and clothing was a familiar routine. I had a couple of worn-out uniforms that I would proudly wear to school.

I cannot give an exact estimate of how far my primary school was from my home, but it's about a forty-five-minute drive one way. Imagine a young girl having to walk such a distance, and often on an empty stomach. What made it worse was that I would usually not have any lunch or money to buy lunch at school. This became so unbearable that I latched on to a couple of girls whom I had known to skip school for reasons that weren't known to me.

I saw that they were happy not being in class, and they always had money to buy snacks, so it was enticing. Like them, I began to skip school and hang out at a waterside place, which provided solitude. For me, this was a great escape. In those moments, I was a kid.

Also, at this place I could reflect on an area of my life that I didn't fully understand. As I would listen to the girls talk about their families, boys, and other matters, I remember so vividly wanting to talk about what had happened to me when I lived in the home where I was born. Although I did not have a full understanding of those events at the time, the memories would not leave me.

In my solitude, I thought about what those adult males had done to me when I was very young. In my mind, I would replay many of the tricks these brothers used to lure me to the back of their apartment. There, on different occasions, each would take turns molesting me. They both raped me time and time again, ignoring the fact that I was a child. To be accurate, I was younger than six years old. It was as if my subconscious was trying to force these memories out of me, as I hadn't been able to forget them.

I did not discuss these incidents with the girls, though, nor with my family or anyone else, for that matter. Instead, I've kept it to myself throughout the years.

As the girls and I socialized, I was aware that I was not doing the right thing by sneaking around. The freedom I had during these times clouded my judgment. Moreover, the girls would share their Tombi and Grunsup with me, which are to this day a few of my favorite African foods. At home, I could almost never afford to have them. So, perhaps now you understand why not going to class was somewhat liberating.

Also, going to school, in my opinion, was sort of the same thing as being at home. At school, I was expected to learn on my own with the other children that were in my class. It was an unpleasant experience, because I learned nothing from my teachers. They could not be effective, because they, too, lacked the proper education. I knew this very well, because all we would do as students, for the most part, was talk to one another and play. Of course, there were a few lessons here and there, but nothing of substance that captivated my attention enough to make me want to attend, as I should have.

Even so, I gained some valuable lessons that only being born and raised for a short while in Freetown would help shape the rest of my journey.

I hinted earlier that my brother and I were scapegoats of Creoledom. Nevertheless, he was the apple of Mamma's eye. He could do no wrong, as far as Mamma was concerned. While I had my uncle's TLC, he had Mamma's. She doted on him, spoiling him rotten. I was so jealous of him, mainly because no one held him to the same level of expectation as me. I guess the saying is right: "Boys are boys and girls are girls."

My brother had a playful life comprised of many friends, while I, on the other hand, had only three friends, girls who held the same responsibilities as me. We had very little playtime, because they, too, were helpers to their families.

He was often away from home, only showing up at mealtime (when we could afford it). Yes, there were many instances when we went without food. He and I often fought, too, but it never lasted for a full day. He loved me and was very protective of me. He knew I played a valuable role in our family, but he didn't know how to support me in that role, because at the time, none of us had a father figure to model after. Mamma's husband had passed away. Although Uncle Kofi supported us, he, too, was a young man who had not developed the necessary parental skills to guide us thoroughly.

In the end, Bollo—which was what his friends nicknamed him, but his name was Richmond—had my back. We spent many nights playing stone ball, our favorite game, and a few other games we played as children when time permitted.

Interestingly, we never went to bed mad at each other, a practice that still exists between my siblings and me. We were blessed to have had Richmond, who passed away in December of 2004 at the tender age of thirty. I was exceptionally blessed to have had him as a big brother and to have shared so many experiences up until when I left home. He had my heart!

I mentioned earlier that Mamma had placed me with her oldest son, my Uncle Sonny, and his family. I believed his willingness to take me in was partly an effort to support us, as he had been financially supportive of Mamma from time to time. As a child, I knew he only gave to his mother just what he thought was sufficient to keep her afloat. He never really cared for my mother, his baby sister, and so he didn't bother to make us his priority. Sonny and my mother never formed a relationship like siblings should.

Nevertheless, I know for a fact that my mother loved him. This assumption became apparent when in the end, he needed my mother's support.

Uncle Sonny and his family had adopted the Creoledom way of living and thinking. When I lived with them, it became clear that I did not belong there, partly because his wife came from a prestigious family, and my being there was uncomfortable for her. She had her picture-perfect family and desired to maintain the standard of living she was accustomed to living.

Also, she never wanted me around her young infant children, because she felt that I came from an underprivileged home. Therefore, I lacked the qualities she had desired for someone who would be associating with her young children. My aunty made it her priority to make my life miserable by demanding that I change my overall appearance and my way of speaking, among other things. Her demands of me were so unrealistic that my failure to meet her expectations would result in her physically beating me. She failed to understand that up until then I had not been exposed to her way of living. She would at times recognize that I lacked what she expected of me, but never rationalized that her request for me to only speak English to her sons was unrealistic. Mind you, no one had ever taught me before then how to speak English.

I was not even a teenager yet at that time. Also, I attended a primary school where Krio was the language we spoke. My family and I also spoke Krio at home. She, on the other hand, had been exposed to a privileged lifestyle. Both of her sons were born in England. I was born in Freetown—Passonage Street, to be exact, which many would call "the hood."

It came to a point where I could not mentally or emotionally endure all I was being forced to face, so I pleaded with Mamma to let me return home, to which she obliged.

Uncle Sonny's wife's account of what caused my return home differs significantly from mine. This bothered me so badly that I would sometimes challenge her to a face-to-face conversation about the facts. I was determined to prove the reality of my experience when I had lived in her home, but as time went on, I began to realize that we all remember our truths based on our account of the events—a rationalization I concluded to be partly due to our subjective way of processing our experiences.

I resolved the issue by burying it for good. To Uncle Sonny's credit, he was never around much, as he frequently traveled in pursuit of their happiness. Moreover, I don't believe he would have treated me the way his wife did, or that he would have allowed her to treat me the way she did. In the end, he became aware of it all—a truth that I know he partly resented based on our conversations later in life.

I shared earlier that my brother Richmond died. To be exact, he passed away on December 29, 2004. I remember the day that my Uncle Sonny called with Richmond in the car as he was being transported to another hospital, because Richmond was gravely ill. Earlier in the day, he had been at another hospital, but he could not be diagnosed adequately there. And so, he was ordered to go somewhere else.

My Uncle Sonny had kept in touch with me on Richmond's progress (or lack thereof), because he knew how close he and I were. On one of those calls, I asked to speak with him. He got on the phone, and we talked briefly. I told him that I loved him. I ordered him to get well and return to his position as the man of the house. To this day, it's unfathomable that our conversation that day would be our last.

Richmond died shortly after arriving at the hospital where my Uncle Sonny had taken him for further evaluation, not long after our conversation. As it turned out, he had been suffering for weeks prior, but had failed to share his symptoms with anyone. Richmond had not been able to use the bathroom at all and had been gaining weight, which many had attributed to his weightlifting. No one had concluded that he had been suffering from kidney failure. A lack of proper diagnosis is a common problem in my country due to the lack of trained medical professionals. Per Mamma's teaching, we accepted Richmond's death and honored God's timing, just as we had learned to do when life dealt us an unforeseen event.

When Richmond died, I was lost at first. I cried for days at a time, mainly because I knew he and I had unfinished business. We had talked about our plans, dreams, and hopes for our futures. Although he, too, had his challenges that I would dare to attribute to his environment, he was optimistic about everything. He did not let poverty hinder his promises, as he saw far into the future by the way he spoke. He was smart, but reserved. He was a lot like our mother in this regard.

I felt like God had not been fair to me. Three months prior, God had taken Mamma from us. So soon after that, three months to be exact, He took Richmond. My math was not adding up with God's. He had blessed me with my daughter that same year. My daughter was six months old when Mamma died and nine months old when her Uncle Richmond died.

Grief consumed me. I mourned my losses while being a new mother. It broke me that neither Richmond nor Mamma would get to meet my daughter. Nevertheless, I persevered, as I had learned to do.

My family has encountered many losses. My baby sister, Christiana, only had a few years with us. Mamma had decided to give her to her biological father in hopes that she would have a better life. The day that Mamma and I took her to Lungi is blurry, as I was just a child myself. The journey was lonely. It was clear that there was going to be a sense of loss. I knew that Christiana was not coming back with us, and she did not.

As we took transportation from Brima Lane, which was where we lived, to Ferry Junction, there was an eerie feeling amongst us, almost as if Mamma was dialoguing with herself, conflicted with her decision. The atmosphere was unpleasant, but we made it to Lungi, which was where Christiana's father worked and lived.

The atmosphere was still out of the ordinary. In my mind and with voices playing in my head, I knew Christiana was only a child who needed security, but I did not blame Mamma for her decision, because I knew Mamma was hoping that Christiana would have what she couldn't afford to give her.

It was a long trip from where the ferry left us to the airport where Christiana's dad worked. From what I can remember, it was a brief conversation between Mamma and Mr. Christopher, Christiana's father, as he took his daughter in his arms. It was almost as if Christiana realized something was wrong. Immediately after that, she began to cry hysterically. For a very long time, I could not erase her screams, nor could I wipe away tears as I thought of her desperate pleas for Mamma not to leave her. She cried uncontrollably to no avail. Instead, he rushed her off, and she disappeared with him.

I remember crying, but I didn't know what part I could play in bringing her back home. Eventually, we left, and life returned to the usual, except that Christiana was no longer a part of us. Neither Mamma nor I knew that that would be the last time we would see her.

Upon our return home, I continued in my role, but with one fewer, and so did the rest of my clan. My mother would visit Christiana from time to time in Bo, which was where she had moved to be with her father's family. Bo is one of the provinces in Sierra Leone. From what I understood, my mother had somewhat of a relationship with Christiana up until the time war broke out in Sierra Leone, and no one could account for her. The rest of us hadn't seen her except hearing stories from what my mother would relate after her visits.

It became clear to me several years later that Christiana had died, because she came to me in a dream to tell me that she was no longer with us. By now, it has been over two decades since anyone has seen or heard from her. I shared her message with my family, but my mother has yet to come to terms with her death, partly because of guilt.

We do not have a full account of what happened to her. However, we have resolved and accepted her death, just as we had the previous ones. Although my mother still struggles to come to terms with her daughter Christiana's passing, my brothers and I have been encouraging her to let go and pray instead for her soul to continue to rest in peace, rather than holding on as if she's still out there somewhere.

My mother has many burdens that she carries—this I know very well—but I believe God has forgiven her. She now has to forgive herself. I am playing an instrumental role in this by being compassionate toward her. I have lowered my expectations of her and have been more giving. We are striving in the right direction.

Like my sister Christiana, I, too, was given to my father, but for me it was around the age of fourteen. I did not participate much in this planning, nor was I aware of all the details. Everything happened so fast that what I retained was my having to meet two new older men (presumably siblings from my father's side), my father's new wife, and an aunt and her children, who were my cousins. Of course, I was polite through it all, but to this day I have not formed any sustainable bond with them. I already had a family, and I was not in search of acquiring any other. I was complete.

Mamma and my father had planned that I would go live with him in Italy. The day of my departure came very quickly. One early morning in the month of October 1989, a car came to pick me up. I honestly don't remember everyone who came along to the airport to give his or her proper sendoffs. Like my sister, it was my turn to go away, and Lungi was the same spot where parts of our destinies connected.

I was amongst strangers: my brothers, my father's sister, and my father's new wife, who was half his age. My aunt's children stayed behind and were scheduled to join us later. I was restless. I had pleaded earlier with Mamma to let me stay with her. I had come to value what we had. I had a family unit that was imperfect, but it was my family. I was exhausted with the demands assigned to me, but I was amongst my people. I had come to know love firsthand through my Mamma and uncles' nurturing.

Moreover, there were values and moral characteristics that I knew I needed to develop, and the only person to teach them to me, in my opinion, was my Mamma. It didn't matter to me that we were poor. I was complete. I deserved that security I had known for all of my almost fourteen years on earth. I needed it to stay that way.

Although I pleaded with Mamma to stay, my pleas went unanswered. As with my sister, Mamma was hoping to give me what she could not: a better life. She knew that love alone could not suffice with all the material things we needed, but I don't think she knew how appreciative I was of all that she had given to my siblings and me. Perhaps if she had known, she would not have been so desperate to seek an alternative. Maybe she did, but felt like it was not enough for us. Little did she know that even as a child, I understood that she gave her all. I know this because she was selfless in letting us go, which I know had to have crushed her genuinely.

Mamma blessed me, and she eventually let me go. At that moment, my sense of security vanished. My world altered, so I prepared myself for the unknown.

A few days later, I arrived in Italy with my new family. It took us a while to get there, because we transited in Moscow. I didn't know these people. I had not formed any relationships with them, and there I was, the youngest of them all. I had to regain my composure and focus quickly on the reasons why Mamma had sacrificed in letting me go. I assumed my position as Mamma's daughter—that is, a critical thinker, humble servant, and compassionate and empathetic daughter who was ready to serve with humility.

I quickly became what Mamma was to our Krio relatives: a helper to my new family by cleaning and doing everyone's laundry. Although my father had a wife, she was very ill—an illness that, on most occasions, prevented her from assuming her role as a wife. Most of her duties fell to me.

My brothers and aunt quickly began working at a factory, so their time at home was limited. I was enrolled in middle school eventually, but that did not limit my father's expectations of me, or that of his wife and my brothers. I felt like a servant rather than a child newly assimilated to the family.

I served without complaining. I had learned from the best, after all. I navigated my role with integrity, as I did not want to disappoint them. I was campaigning for a secure position that would enable me to assimilate smoothly. Alas, my attempts never really materialized.

My aunt and father acted as if they had some old, unfinished business. It was very uncomfortable to be around them. While my father seemed more open and friendly, my aunt was reserved, and she very seldom interacted with my father, which was something I felt was unordinary. Nevertheless, they were adults, and it was their issue, not mine.

My aunt moved out fairly quickly and got her own place, as she had been able with my father's help to bring her children to join her. Shortly after that, my father decided to return to his native province of Bo, Sierra Leone.

By now, it was clear that my new beginning was uncertain. I did not have a close relationship with my aunt or my brothers, and I knew very little about my stepmother. I barely even knew my father, because he had not been around, not even when I was born, which caused my maternal great-grandfather to legitimize me. Before my arrival in Italy, he had visited with me briefly in Freetown a few times, but that was about the extent of our relationship.

Coincidentally, one of those visits was also when he had to establish paternity of me by signing an affidavit stating that I was his biological child. This is the reason there's an addition to my birth certificate that I am also required to produce when dealing with legal matters, as my last name on my original birth certificate is Wellington.

I was baffled that within a relatively short period, he decided that he was relocating. *What?* My mind started to wonder, *What are his plans for me? Who will assume responsibility of me?* The answers to these questions came before I asked them out loud when my father approached me with his idea.

He had arranged for my aunt to take care of me. I would move in with her and her daughters in their new place, which was within walking distance from our home. My brothers and my father's wife would stay and assume the responsibility of the house. Again, being Mamma's daughter, I am rationalizing his idea in my head while trying to make sense of it all. I couldn't help but wonder if he, too, had not formed the parental skills needed to bond with his children, because by then he had a couple more sons with his new wife. They were infants when he decided to return home.

I mean, for Pete's sake. The man did not know any of us. He had just made the ultimate sacrifice in bringing all of us to Italy in hopes of a better future. Wouldn't he have wanted to stay a while longer and get to know his adult sons, his young daughter, his infant sons, and his new wife, whom he did not know at all due to their marriage being arranged? It did not appear to be the case in any of our regards. For his infant sons, my father had planned to give custody of them to a couple of Italian families prior to his departure for Bo.

By now, he had the plan for his life, which didn't include any of us. My father eventually left us in Italy with his plan for our lives in motion. Fortunately for my stepmother and younger brothers, they were able to visit with my father in Bo shortly after his departure for home. Their visit was brief, and they returned to Italy before the war broke. Upon their return, my younger brothers went to live with their respective custodial parents.

I could say with all certainty that that was the last time my father ever saw his wife and sons. My father's explanation was that he had been exhausted from working hard-labor jobs. His choice for bringing us to Italy would be that the adults could now help support him. He also had a vision for a project that he was banking on upon his return home. Sadly, his dream quickly dissipated, partly due to the war, which started not too long after he arrived. Also, none of his perfectly crafted plans (that included help from his sister and older sons) materialized, as they were (and still are) as selfish as they can be.

As my father had instructed, I moved in with my aunt. Funnily, this living arrangement, like the previous two in Freetown, did not succeed. My aunt wanted her children to be like me, from what I could assess. This was the case mostly for the oldest. My aunt would frequently compare everything I did to her oldest daughter. It appeared they had a relationship that was already fragile, in which she felt that her daughter had disappointed her. Her older daughter was a few years older than me, but I demonstrated the level of tenacity and grit that my aunt desired in her daughter.

It was uncomfortable to be around.

To make matters worse, she invited my first boyfriend to her house to ask him for financial support to help care for me. Her reason was that my father had left me with her with no financial backup. Seriously? I barely knew the young man! It was a teenage love, and he was still getting to know me.

I decided to move out, and returned to the home of my stepmother and brothers. Well, I couldn't distinguish which was worse: being at my aunt's or returning home. The circumstances were the same. Nonetheless, unbeknownst to my father and the rest of my newfound family, I had a plan in motion, which is something I take no credit for orchestrating. In my mind, my Mamma's prayers were always at work on my behalf, because even though life was an uphill battle in Italy, almost all of my endeavors came to fruition.

I had formed friendships with several other adults, mainly older people who owned businesses. We lived in a small town that was very productive regarding work. I had been soliciting work, even though I was not of legal age to work yet. I was seeking employment not because I had financial obligations to my brothers and stepmother—well, so I thought—but rather to help take care of my family back home in Freetown and to support myself. I was responsible for me, because no one else would take account of what I needed.

Through what I thought were Mamma's prayers, I got a job working under the table at a factory. I worked in the afternoon after I arrived home from middle school. I don't remember the specific hours, but I know I worked up until around 9 or 10 p.m. I didn't complain much, instead keeping my focus on what was important. I was making progress.

I began to earn my living. I contributed to my family's wellbeing back home. However, something happened shortly after that that changed my course. My older brothers approached me with a demand that I start to pay three hundred lira per month for living there with them. Mind you, they were both working and had live-in girlfriends. My stepmother worked only periodically due to her health. Yet, I did not question their decision, but obliged instead.

Interestingly, I did not have my own room in the house, because they were all occupied. I slept in the living room, making my bed on the floor wherever I felt comfortable. I endeavored, though, while I strategized my next move.

Having been raised the way I had been, there was no way I could have continued living there, paying them three hundred lira a month, and being their maid, as my household duties did not subside. Their decision to treat me, a child, like an adult and not support me, as they should have, caused a considerable strain in our relationship.

It became a blessing that one of my brothers had a girlfriend who was older than him. She became a mother figure to me. I also had a cousin who had joined us in Italy and was living with us, along with my brother's girlfriend's sister. All three of us slept on the floor in the living room.

There were times when things were rough, even in Italy. We had to manage as best as we could. In doing so, we became a support system for each other. Although my brother's girlfriend, her sister, and my cousin were older than me, they did not treat me as if I were lesser than; they embraced me and became my mentors and support system.

As the years went on, I continued to work various jobs. I worked at a factory, as a housekeeper in a hotel, as kitchen staff in several restaurants (primarily responsible for doing the dishes), as a maid for multiple families, as well as live-in staff to an elderly couple.

Yes, like in Freetown, my desire for an education plummeted. I did poorly at school and barely graduated middle school. Upon graduation, my final grade was a "sufficiency," which was part of their grading scale. At that time, everything about my life in Italy resembled that of Freetown, except I was partly responsible for aiding adults in their activities of daily living, and I could earn a living.

I also moved around on several occasions with my support

system, because by then my older brother's relationship with Gigi, as we called her, had dissolved. Gigi, her sister, and my cousin seemed to end up at the same place almost always, so I would still end up in the same area as they were, until I began to strategize my next move. I forfeited going to high school, because work had become my priority. I needed to survive. My family back home required my financial assistance, and I could not let them down.

As I continued with life in Italy, it became apparent that I was destined for more. Don't ask how the realization came to be. Something inside of me began to shift. It was clear to see that my pulse had started to beat at a pace it never had before. Ideas flowed in my head, and desires began to manifest in my heart. My position shifted. I was changing. I was maturing. I still didn't know what awaited me and what my newfound perspectives of life were all about, but I adhered to my beating pulse.

I began to move at a different pace. I applied myself in everything I did. I started to let go of my childish ways, gravitating instead toward a more mature way of thinking, which caused an issue between my boyfriend and me. Yes, that same boy my aunt had summoned to be financially responsible for me had also become somewhat of my guardian angel. He was my first love. He taught me many things. He even showed me how to drive. Well, as I began to gain my footing, he felt less effective, so we started arguing a lot and eventually went our separate ways. To him, I had become a different person.

My new beginning did not go over so well with many other people. Nevertheless, I did not let that distract me. I remained focused and continued in my pursuits.

You do remember I mentioned that I had made friends with some older adults that had connections, don't you? Well, one of them, it turned out, would play a pivotal role in my life. Vicenzo was his name. Vicenzo's brother and my father were good friends. My father was friends with his entire family. Vicenzo's older brother became inseparable with my older brothers, while I, on the other hand, formed a special bond with Vicenzo, who owned an electronics store. Being raised by a woman who was persistent in obtaining what she wanted, I pestered Vicenzo to death with appeals to hire me as a clerk at his store. The poor man would do his best to explain that he didn't have a need.

Nevertheless, that didn't stop me. I persisted, and Vicenzo eventually gave in, and then my life changed again in what had seemed like a progression. Through my earnings, I was able to visit with my family in Freetown. It had been several years since I had left them. My visit lasted for about a month. It was fulfilling to see Mamma (which turned out to be our last time together), my mother, my siblings, and my other relatives again. Yes, I even saw my father, who visited with me for less than thirty minutes. After he collected the gifts and money I brought him, he cited that he had a more pressing matter to attend to, and so he needed to return to Bo minutes after his arrival in Freetown.

The rest of my family valued our time together. We talked about our lives, among other things. It was a relief for me to have been able to see them again.

As with all things, my visit came to an end, and I returned to Italy. Upon my return, I resumed my normal routine, but continued in my quest for a better life, mainly because I had not continued on to high school. I knew that I wouldn't succeed with only having a middle school education, but for the time being, working offered me security.

At the same time, my cousin (my aunt's older daughter) relocated to London, England, and began to encourage me to relocate there, as well, as she believed that the move would be beneficial to me. After much encouragement from her, I started to plan to move to London.

With my employment at Vicenzo's, I was able to get a visa to England for six months. I worked hard and saved up. I eventually took off for London with hopes for a new beginning. There, it became apparent that it was not where I belonged—an assumption based on the living conditions of the people I stayed with and with whom I associated day to day. Like in Italy, life was rough for them. Privileges were few for immigrants.

I quickly concluded that I would not leave Italy to permanently relocate to London to live a lifestyle similar to what I already had. Most importantly, I had developed a burning desire to attain more for myself. Therefore, I returned to Italy and continued in my familiar environment.

If you'll recall, I hinted earlier that something different had sparked inside of me, correct? Well, that feeling did not leave me. It became vividly alive, and it was as if someone else were living inside of me attempting to navigate the rest of my journey. It didn't feel like I was a part of the process, but I had no objection to what was happening in my life.

While I continued in the workforce, I contemplated what would enable me to achieve those things that were festering inside of me. Eventually, Vicenzo presented me with an opportunity to travel with him and his family to America on a business trip. I thought to myself, *The man is out of his mind.* I would not be able to get a visa to travel because, at the time, it was difficult for immigrants to get a visa except under extenuating circumstances. I knew this firsthand, as many adults were applying to no avail.

Moreover, I didn't know much about America, and so I was not hyped. However, Vicenzo continued planning and did something that was unheard of.

One afternoon while I was at the shop, he handed me a folder containing all of the supporting documentation I would need to obtain my visa. Wait a minute! This man was giving me all of his banking and business information, and ordering me to go to Rome and apply for a visa. There was not much that I could say, so I complied. After all, he was the boss.

In the end, I got on a train headed to Rome, and did as he had ordered me to do. In my mind, I had no expectation of gaining an approval based on what I'd heard from the adults who'd attempted to get a visa to America.

The journey was about six to seven hours one way from where I lived. Finally, I arrived safely in Rome. I asked for directions to the embassy, as that was my first time visiting Rome. I meticulously made my way to the embassy, but not before briefly sightseeing, as the city was one that I had never seen before. However, I regrouped and remembered my reason for being there. I walked to the embassy, a distance that seemed like forever. Upon my arrival there, it was clear that I was a teenager; I was overly friendly and asked many questions. Ultimately, the time came for me to complete the paperwork and present my file, which I did.

I remember that the interview was brief and comprised of questions like, What was I going to America for, and with whom? How long had I been in Italy, and what was my profession? I answered all of the questions. I distinctly remember the interviewer asking if Vicenzo was my boyfriend. My goodness! He was old enough to be my father.

The interviewer eventually asked that I return a few hours later that same afternoon, but took my passport from me. I left and returned to sightseeing, but kept watch on the clocks that were visible at every corner of the city. I was determined not to miss my afternoon appointment.

With diligence, I made it back a few minutes early. As faith would have it, the interviewer and I met in the elevator on our way up. He spoke Italian fluently, so we interacted. He acted as if he had known me for a while. I reciprocated his niceness and applied myself by being equally as lovely as he had been to me.

We made our way in, and he motioned for me to sit and wait. All the while, I believed I was in a daze. Nothing made sense of how the day was going. It seemed too smooth and productive. While these thoughts played in my head, the interviewer interrupted me by handing me back my passport as if to say, "Approved."

Say what now?

I opened my passport and looked at the green stamp, then I extended my gratitude and left. On my way down, an older black man with what I assumed to be a British accent asked if I had gotten a visa. I responded yes. He asked to see my passport, and I complied. He took a look at it and noticed that there had been an error. He directed me back into the office for them to make the necessary corrections. He must have worked there, too, I concluded.

I did as he asked of me. This mistake caused me to wait again a little while longer. In the end, I left with a visa that met all the qualifications to travel. I got on the train and returned home. I kept looking at my passport, amazed at what had happened.

As soon as I returned home, I related what had happened and shared that I had gotten a visa. Because it was late and Vicenzo had gone for the day, I waited until the next day and went to the shop to show him my passport. I don't remember asking about their travel plans, as he was directing all of it, so I concluded he had their ducks in the row.

Sadly, soon after, Vicenzo's life took a tragic turn. His wife passed away unexpectedly. Now, our travel plan was on hold.

During this time, one of my brothers saw an opportunity in me having gotten a visa and was instrumental in ensuring that I did not waste what many had considered a blessing. He talked to me about the possibility of coming to America on my own, and arranged for my accommodation once I arrived. I knew I had to discuss it with Vicenzo and gain his approval, and so I shared with Vicenzo my conversation with my brother. He did not object. I was grateful! Recognizing his generosity, before my departure, I mourned his loss and supported his little children as best I could.

As with my departure from Freetown, my leaving from Italy to America seemed immediate. My brother, the one who had talked me into moving, drove me to the airport. By then, we had formed something of a relationship. Before this point, I had vowed to always keep him at arm's length. My brother had abused me physically, beating me as no one had ever done before. Sure, I got a whooping while I was home in Freetown, but my Uncle Kofi, the only male who disciplined me, was gentle in his approach. But with my brothers, they were treating me like an adult, and so, I decided to respond as such. On many occasions, this brother and I would butt heads, which would result in him putting his hands on me.

I still remember one time when he decided to lay his hands on me, and I was on my period. He swept me off my feet by kicking both of my feet so hard that I fell to the floor and my pad flew off. It was then that I decided that he would never entirely be a part of me. Although he had been instrumental in the planning of my leaving Italy, our relationship has always been on the as-needed basis.

Because of our history, I was still numb emotionally. Therefore, when he drove me to the airport, I didn't particularly feel the level of sadness he demonstrated. He began to talk to me as he had never done before. He even shared how much he loved me. In that moment, all I was replaying in my head was what he and my other brother had failed to do on my behalf. Guilt must have kicked in, and his conscience was eating at him. I was not at the same emotional level with him, however, so I participated less in the conversation and gave very little in return.

Once we made it to the airport, which was over an hour's drive, he cried as I made my way through security. I was not able to see past what he had done to me, mainly because I felt victimized by someone who was supposed to have cared for me. I am grateful, though, to him for inspiring me to move and arranging that I would be taken care of once I arrived in the US, but otherwise, not much has changed since then between us.

If you perhaps are wondering what role my other older brother played in my life, the answer may surprise you. He was similar to my other brother, but had always made me uncomfortable because of the way he looked at me. Something about his demeanor caused me to be on guard when I was around him.

The sense of uneasiness I felt had come full circle one day at a house party at our friend's home. Everyone had been having a good time and dancing. I was sitting down with one of my friends when he approached and asked me to dance. He pulled me up and led me to the dance floor. As we began to dance, he got closer and closer, something I felt was odd for an older brother. As I attempted to back away from him, he extended his hand and reached down under my skirt in an attempt to touch my vagina. He grabbed me through my clothes, but I pulled back, smacked his hand, and walked away. They had dimmed the lights, so the dance floor had been dark. His behavior caused what would be my last encounter with him. To this day, I have not spoken to him, nor have I seen him. He still lives in Italy, from what I know.

In regard to the rest of my "Italian family," my stepmother passed away a few years ago. I did not keep in contact with her, because we had never developed a bond. One of my younger brothers, Piero, also died a couple of years ago. Piero and I never got an opportunity to know one another, because he and his older brother James were raised by their Italian families. My aunt and her children are in the US.

Through the passing of Piero, I was able to reconnect with my other brother, James. The death of Piero brought James and me to a place we would have never imagined possible. Of course, at first we interacted like strangers, but over time, he and I have come to love one another. I took my daughter to Italy to meet him last year, and we spent some quality time together. He, in turn, visited with us this past summer, along with one of our older brother's sons (the one who encouraged me to move).

Like with James and Piero, I had not developed a relationship with Lorenzo, who was around the age of one when I relocated to America. This past summer, though, we got to make up for lost time.

Prior to my departure to the US, Lorenzo, my nephew whom we nicknamed Renzo, had regarded me as his mother. We had a very close bond during the first year of his life. Renzo would follow me around and cry whenever I would leave to go somewhere. He even slept with me, and on many occasions would ignore his mother. Renzo's mother, Amie, had also been a support system to me, just as Gigi had been. Amie was instrumental in helping my brother arrange for my relocation to the US.

It was refreshing to mend these relationships. Both James and Lorenzo are now part of my life, and I maintain contact with Gigi, Amie, and all of the other women who had played such an essential role in my life.

I now conclude that everything that happened to me happened so that I would not be comfortable settling at those initial stages. God had many untapped territories that I still needed to uncover.

Chapter Three

Coming to America

Forgetting those things which are behind, and reaching forth unto those things which are before.
—Philippians 3:13 (KJV)

I arrived in America on November 21, 1995, a few months shy of my twentieth birthday and one day shy of what many Americans consider one of the biggest holidays in the country: Thanksgiving. I wasn't quite sure why my new host family was eager to arrive home on time after picking me up from the airport. They had much unfinished planning, as they were hosting Thanksgiving Day that year, something that they shared with me later on. It was a day full of adventure. Thankfully, the adults spoke Krio.

When I arrived, I was not on guard, because my new host family was related to my brother's girlfriend, Amie. Moreover, on a few occasions before my arrival, I had spoken with them via telephone. They seemed nice. When I arrived, they welcomed me with open arms. I felt like I belonged.

The wife was a nursing student, while the husband was a cab driver. They had two small children: a girl around the age of five and a boy around three. They represented something I'd never had before: a nuclear family unit. I was pleased to be around something that was different for a change.

Then came the day, November 22, 1995. Fully prepared, the family hosted several friends for the big occasion. Their home was full of a mixed crowd comprised of elders, young adults, and children. It was a wonderful celebration, and I got to experience what Thanksgiving is all about: people acknowledging their blessings and being grateful for what they have been able to accomplish throughout the year. I fit right in, as I was even more thankful than any of them could imagine.

I had gained a fresh start. My life was just beginning in the US of A.

At first, there was not much that I could do upon my arrival in the US, because I needed to get my ducks in a row, which presented an opportunity for my host family. For the first few months, I stayed home and babysat the little boy, who was not of school age. We got along just fine, as he was delightful. I was also responsible for picking the little girl up from the bus stop when she returned home from school, as her parents would still be at work at that time. This arrangement worked out fine. I felt like I was contributing, considering that I could not afford to pay them financially.

Things went smoothly for quite some time, as we all seemed to fit in our roles. Eventually, with their assistance, I was able to gain employment at McDonald's.

I knew a little bit about McDonald's from Italy, because my former boyfriend and I would go there at least once a month for a date night. I was not all that concerned about my inability to speak English proficiently. I didn't think it would be required, because after all, I'd only be serving food.

Well, as with many things before, my assumption was wrong. Management assumed that I spoke English very well. Therefore, my first assignment was working the drive-thru. I kid you not! Imagine me working the drive-thru at a McDonald's. Lo and behold, disaster was imminent. Chaos is what it became. I am smiling as I write this paragraph, because it was by the grace of God that my employment continued there for as long as it did.

As confident as I was in my ability to serve, my lack of proficiency in the language prevented me from mastering the position adequately, so it caused me to be moved around often. For this, I was thankful. I had three guardian angels there. One was a manager, Joe, and the other two were the brothers of one of the girls I had befriended at the Thanksgiving Day party. She, too, played a part, as my host family was instrumental in me getting the job. Joe quickly became my support, while the other manager was sick of having to babysit me. I failed miserably at verbally serving. I only knew the necessary English words to get by, but not to work in an environment where it was required.

Nevertheless, my hands could work diligently, which was something Joe observed. He encouraged me to join the kitchen crew preparing the food versus working the drive-thru. I was thrilled. I didn't enjoy working the drive-thru, because people were mean and unforgiving. I had lines that backed up to what seemed like miles away. The customers would complain about my accent, among other things.

Yes, I also needed to learn how to calculate the money. Recognizing my shortcomings, I welcomed Joe's suggestion. I joined Jr. and Paul (my friend's brothers), and the rest of the kitchen crew comprised of young men. There, I excelled. I fit right in, and I was comfortable. I became a professional burger flipper and egg scrambler. I was on a roll.

With the support of Joe and the boys, I was able to thrive. They had my back and would defend me on many occasions when some of my coworkers, who were teenage girls and young adults themselves, were rude and nasty. They had come to believe that I required too much attention to work a job that they considered easy. I would argue with them often, because I did not want them to think that they could push me around. With my broken English, I stood up for myself, and Paul would, too. He defended me fiercely.

Jr., on the other hand, was shy and reserved. Even so, he provided me with emotional support, mostly in private. I later concluded that he, too, had felt some level of uneasiness with the girls, but he remained a gentleman.

Joe became my English teacher, also. He would often correct me when my grammar or pronunciation differed from what it should've been. Joe was determined to help me, and so he did an excellent job at mentoring me.

There was another manager with whom I sometimes worked. His name was Marc. Marc, unlike Joe, did not show the level of empathy I needed. He was bothered by how much time he needed to invest on my behalf while on duty.

By now, Joe had moved me to the front registers. I had become a cashier. Marc would verbally redirect me in front of customers and my peers in such a rude way that I would often feel insecure. He lacked discretion, and he had a temper. The combination of the two prevented him from being an effective supervisor. Marc was not only mean toward me, but with others whom he felt were incompetent. Several girls quit under Marc's leadership. I, on the other hand, could not afford to leave. I stayed and endured. I was determined to ride the course—until the unthinkable happened.

I arrived at work one afternoon to what had been an investigation into me. Marc had reported that my register was short the day prior. Mind you, everyone working as a cashier must reconcile his or her cash register before leaving at the end of the shift, something I was 100 percent certain that I did. I had no problem, because I counted every penny before I submitted my end-of-shift report. I was baffled.

I began to sweat. I didn't know what had happened. All I could do was explain that I submitted the correct report along with every penny. Marc, on the other hand, concluded that he didn't want to hear my explanation and that he had made his decision. He handed me a piece of paper to sign. In it, Marc had decided to suspend me for three days. Most humiliating of all, he did not do this in the back office, but rather in front of other people.

I felt crushed and humiliated. I was disappointed, because I knew with all certainty I had not taken money from my register and that I had submitted everything correctly to Marc before leaving at the end of my shift. Unfortunately, I could not defend myself, so I went home and was off for the next three days.

By then, I had moved out of my host home and was rooming with Paul, Jr., and Jenny, my friend from Thanksgiving. My living arrangement with my host family had begun to change. The wife had become accustomed to me being responsible for the children, and so had attempted to limit my work schedule. I rebelled by not adhering to her demands, so we clashed. I did not relocate to America to only assume the role of a babysitter; I had come to earn a better living and to make a life for myself.

At my new place, I roomed with Paul. Yes, we slept in the same bed. Funnily, we would often act like real siblings by the way we fought. Paul had become my Richmond. We matched perfectly. Paul was partially responsible for my tomboyish attitude. He was skinny, so I would wear his gym pants and baseball caps often. He never complained.

While Paul and I bonded, Jr. developed a crush on me. His desire was something I was unable to reciprocate, but it never interfered in our friendship. Jr. was calm. He indeed was a gentleman. He, too, helped me with most of what I needed.

Jenny served as a big sister for all of us. She assumed the responsibility of everything: grocery shopping, bills, and all else, literally. Up until then, I had been independent, so I did not adequately invest in what Jenny was expecting of me. She had divided the rent equally and the amount we all would contribute toward the necessary items for the household. I felt uneasy with her decision to run everything. Yes, I opened my big mouth and shared my position. My decision to question and offer any input on how the household should run caused a strain, but we were able to continue living together for a while longer.

I eventually returned to work after my suspension, but I had lost all of my interest in being there. I was not the same staff member who had left. My enthusiasm had faded. Thankfully, my dearest Joe was once again at my side. He told me not to be discouraged. Like Paul and Jr., Joe had also suspected that Marc had made up the story to get me to resign. Joe concluded that he trusted me.

I was pleased with their level of compassion toward me. I felt loved and cared for by these gentlemen. Nevertheless, I knew I couldn't continue working at McDonald's, so I began looking for employment elsewhere—Bojangles', to be exact.

After much planning and doing all that I needed to do to be employed there, I got the job. I submitted my resignation to McDonald's and was ready to spread my wings once more. Without question, it was a difficult decision to leave what I had come to know as a work-support system, but I could not continue being there, partly because I was afraid of what Marc or the women would come up with next.

At Bojangles', my immediate supervisor was from Nigeria. He quickly took a liking to me when I shared that I was from Sierra Leone. As faith would have it, he, too, became protective of me. He helped me a lot by mentoring me and at times allowing me to work overtime hours, among other favors. Like Joe, he understood the need to be a role model to all of his employees, and he was respectful. I worked at Bojangles' for quite some time, until I relocated to Wisconsin.

At home, my living arrangement continued with my roommates. By now, I had a love interest that I had been set up with by another friend whom I met at the Thanksgiving Day party. It was as if both ladies were destined to play a part in my life. She had decided that I would make an excellent girlfriend for a friend of hers, so she connected us.

He lived in Wisconsin, so for a while, it was a long-distance relationship. We primarily communicated via telephone before he eventually came to visit with me in Charlotte. He was a handsome hunk, and we matched well together.

We dated for about a year while taking turns visiting each other. Like me, he was from Sierra Leone, which allowed us to bond even faster, and we had some similarities. Through time, I came to befriend one of his sisters and other good friends of his. We had something special there, I thought, until it became apparent that he had been cheating on me. Even then, we tried to make the relationship work, but I was not as invested as I had been, because I felt betrayed.

We eventually separated. I continued to focus on work, until love found me again. Yes, another connection. This one was set up by an acquaintance. He lived locally, so things were different at first.

As I basked in my new love interest, I decided to move out of Jenny's place. I needed to be as independent as I had been, which I didn't feel was possible if I had to room with the others. Paul and I contemplated getting our own place. Eventually, I concluded that it would be wrong to steal Paul away from Jenny, because it had been the three of them before my arrival. I also considered her financial dependency on her brothers, so I discouraged Paul from moving with me.

Instead, I welcomed the invitation by my reasonably new boyfriend to room with him and his sister. They had a two-bedroom apartment, so he convinced me that it was a good idea. I weighed the pros and cons, and finally I agreed.

I am embarrassed to share that things did not go as I had anticipated. He quickly became possessive and controlling. It also became apparent that his need for me to move in was because he needed my financial support to make ends meet. Furthermore, I learned later that he, too, had been cheating on me. Moreover, he was in love with the other woman, who was also in a relationship at the time, so she could not fully reciprocate his affection. I had become the substitute, which played a part in the way he treated me. Things got very ugly between us.

As I endured what was going on at home, I strategized to move out of state. I had come to like Wisconsin. During my visits there, I felt like I belonged. The young adults whom I had befriended seemed to focus on achieving something in their lives. They worked and attended college at the same time. I was impressed with their abilities to multitask.

When my boyfriend put me out after another one of our arguments, I reached out to one of the friends and shared what had happened. Without hesitation, he came to my rescue by agreeing for me to move to Wisconsin. I left that very same day and slept at another friend's home. I also ended up sharing my ordeal with my manager at Bojangles', and sadly resigned without proper notice. Thankfully, he understood.

Within days, I moved to Wisconsin, and another chapter in my life began.

The flight to Wisconsin was short. I was indifferent about having to leave, mostly because of what had transpired. Nevertheless, I was ready to explore what my new chapter entailed, and I arrived open-minded.

It was indeed a fresh start. Upon my arrival at my new home, I was surrounded by young adults with a zest for living and enthusiasm for life. I ended up staying with Junisa, my friend, and his girlfriend, Annie, temporarily. Junisa had been searching for a suitable living arrangement for me, as he and Annie lived in a one-bedroom apartment at the time. It wasn't too long before he paired me up with a friend of his.

Interestingly, it seemed like all of the Sierra Leoneans lived within a few miles of each other. It was a tiny college town, so everyone was basically in each other's backyards. After a brief stay with Junisa and Annie, I moved to a little unit that was very similar to living in a motel. Nonetheless, I was grateful, as it was by a humble gesture that this living arrangement had come to be.

Junisa's friend Ian, as we called him, had agreed to surrender his unit to me while he moved in with another friend of theirs next door. I again thought of my Mamma and how hard she must have been praying on my behalf.

Things were looking up. I was blending in with the young crowd, and they were inspiring me. As I was gaining my wings, my ex—the one from Wisconsin who had cheated on me—began to solicit reconciliation. I had no desire to reconnect, because I was over him. I kept my focus on attaining an education, just like everyone else there was doing. It was a college town, after all, so you could not help but feel compelled to achieve an education.

Nevertheless, I had some challenges. My English was still in its infancy stage. It needed to be improved. With the help of my new friends, I was finally able to enroll at a technical college, where I took some classes. Over time, I became better at speaking and understanding the language, so much so that Junisa was able to connect me to another school, where I enrolled to take the certified nursing-assistant (CNA) course.

Well, let me tell you. This endeavor was no joke. I did well in the practical aspect of things, but failed miserably in the written parts. Yes, I failed on several occasions, and for the life of me I could not pass the final exam, which in turn, prevented me from obtaining the CNA license. But, I had a praying grandmother, so yes, I attributed this next favor to her prayers.

Our instructor was from Russia. She, too, had experienced some of my dilemmas. She shared with me one day when we were alone, and offered to assist me one-on-one with understanding what I needed to know so I could pass the final exam. We began our tutoring sessions late in the afternoon after her lectures. In the end, I took the test and passed with flying colors. I became a certified nursing assistant, and another career began for me, one that I took pleasure in so much that I could not leave work.

I worked for a company that provided support for individuals with autism, mental disabilities, and traumatic brain injuries. It was as if all of the young-adult college students were being recruited to work there. It became a family affair. While almost all of my colleagues were college students, I was a full-time staff member working endlessly.

I had become interested in furthering my education, and so I worked very hard to save money. Thankfully, the need for extra support was always there. I became the staff member whom everyone would call to fill in when there was a need. I remember one of the supervisors pleading with me on many occasions to take a day off. I obliged by going home for a few hours, but returned shortly afterward. Honestly, I worked over one hundred hours every pay period, which was biweekly, almost all of the time.

Work was going very well for me as I bonded with my clients, whom I distinctly remember to this day. They helped develop what Mamma had begun in me. Both required a substantial amount of patience, love, empathy, and compassion. They deserved dignity and respect in spite of the odds.

My clients were both autistics with severe mental challenges and behavioral problems, so many staff members could not successfully work with them, which was partly the reason I was able to work as much as I did. However, it was as if we needed one another. They needed me, and I needed them, so we became inseparable. To them, I had become a family member, one that they did not have because their families were not active in their lives. We did almost everything they enjoyed doing.

In turn, I learned much of what I needed to develop. I became detail-oriented and very observant. They taught me how to appreciate the fundamental differences that exist between humans, particularly those whom society deems unlovable. I developed patience for things and people that previously would have irked me. I learned to be compassionate toward others. Moreover, they inspired me to be empathetic, which is one of the attributes that I am most grateful to have gained from my employment with them.

During this time, I did not socialize much with the others, as I was busy working and they were, too, along with managing their school loads. But, we would occasionally meet at the complex were we all stayed and share some moments of fun.

Junisa was never around much. He was very driven, and so he was always out and about planting his seeds. He knew almost everyone in that small town where we lived. I mean, the guy was like a celebrity. It didn't hurt that he was a handsome hunk, as well. Many girls gravitated toward him. Nevertheless, he was not about that life. His focus was on achieving the goals he had set for himself, one being his desire to further his career. He, too, inspired me to aim for more.

Needless to say, I began to yearn for more, mainly earning a college degree. Yes, a young lady who had only attained a middle school diploma now desired to attain a college education. *Oh, Caspita!* ("Good heavens!" in English.)

Unbeknownst to me, Junisa had inadvertently become a matchmaker, as well. While he was never around, he had commissioned Ian and his buddy Charles to assume the responsibility of me. It was almost as if he had handed me over to Ian. Like with Paul and Jr. in Charlotte, Charles and Ian became my support in Wisconsin. As our friendships grew, Ian and I became an item. He had something I had always longed to have: a devoted father and mother. He was part of a family unit that supported each other, and all of them were reaching for the stars.

Naturally, I became eager to belong. Unfortunately, my need for stability came at a very high cost, as my relationship with Ian was very unhealthy. It was clear that we were not on the same maturity level, and so we would argue a lot. Also, his need for materialism and womanizing played a considerable part in our day-to-day dysfunction. Nevertheless, we were determined to persevere, mostly because I played an essential role in his life.

I had formed a bond with his mother and baby sister. Often, his mother would serve as my emotional compass. I couldn't tell you how many times she devoted herself to me by encouraging me and teaching me to learn how to love her son. She knew I was ten steps ahead of him as it related to maturity, so much so that she would share her own experiences with her husband, Ian's father, in her attempts to get me to be still.

Well, this coping mechanism went on for years. Yes, Ian and I were together for several years. During this time, I endured and sacrificed a lot. I was a part of something that felt right, even though it was apparent that it was an unhealthy place for me. Ian had everything I lacked: a mother, father, and almost all of his siblings in one place. They were happy and healthy. I loved being a part of it, and so I devalued myself. In essence, I became what I was expected to be: submissive.

I served in this role for several years, until an incident occurred that could have changed both of our lives for good. Even then, my desire to belong overshadowed my reality. It wasn't until it became blatantly apparent after our ordeal that he had no desire to change, but most importantly, that he had never respected me. Then, I became determined to leave, so I did.

I moved to a nearby town about twenty minutes away. By then, I was only a few minutes away from work, and so again, I buried myself in my job. Ian's sister and I had become very close, so we maintained our friendship. We became each other's "ride or die," so much so that we became inseparable. Also, my relationship with his mother continued, as well as those with the rest of his siblings.

I continued to work long hours, but was still yearning to further my education. I began to seek advice from Junisa. Through our many days of brainstorming, Junisa developed a plan. One day, he asked that I meet him at the university. I had purchased a car, unlike in Charlotte, where I had been forced to ride public transportation. I adhered to Junisa's request. Little did I know, he had set up a meeting with the university's president.

I told you the man knew everyone and that he had connections!

Upon my arrival, I did not know what was going on, nor could I have imagined what was going to happen. So it became that I was in a meeting with Junisa and the president. Junisa made the introduction to set the stage for me to plead my case. I thought he must have lost his mind. Seriously!

I was nervous. I didn't have the right words, nor did I know what to say. Junisa, with his charming personality, eased the tension, and so I began to talk. Our meeting was brief, but to me, it seemed like it went on for eternity. By the end, the president requested that I bring him all of my school paperwork from Italy.

By all accounts, Junisa has lost his mind, I thought to myself. I reminded him that I had only graduated from middle school. He shared that he had related this information to the president. Can you imagine the look on my face? Shocked.

Despite my insecurities, I submitted the requested information along with a letter of interest, which Junisa helped me to write by the deadline. Shortly after that, I received a letter from the university asking me to take a placement test.

I immediately called Junisa to seek his guidance. Junisa instructed me on what the requirements were and helped guide me on how to go about purchasing the books that I'd need to study with, which I did. I studied for a while and eventually set up the appointment with the testing center to take the placement test. I was not at all confident in my abilities. I was nervous beyond words. I questioned my decision heavily, mainly because I didn't want to look ignorant to the rest of the young adults there.

Nonetheless, I summoned enough courage to walk in and face my fear of failing. After a brief introduction, the test proctor administering the test beckoned me to my seat and explained the requirements. Honestly, I did not retain a word she said to me that day. I was a nervous wreck, but I knew I couldn't turn back; it was happening.

With my No. 2 pencil in hand, I started on my test and completed all of it. Thankfully, I was able to finish within the allocated timeframe, and so I handed my packets back to the test proctor. The feeling of defeat came upon me, because I was sure that I had not done well.

I exited the building and slowly walked to my car. I drove home without telling anyone that I had taken the test—something I kept to myself until Junisa called to inform me that the university president had summoned us to his office. For the love of life, I wondered what the outcome was and why he couldn't mail me the results. *Does he really need Junisa there?*, I asked myself. I had kept this a secret, and now it was all out in the open. I was afraid that Junisa would feel betrayed, because I had not told him that I had taken the test. I had a ready-made explanation for him if he were to ask.

We went to see the president. Just as it was the first time, Junisa began the conversation and eventually eased both the president and me into it. I was grateful that he did not share with the president that he was unaware that I took the test. A sigh of relief came over me as I waited to hear what my results were.

In the meantime, the president kept turning the papers that he held in his hands back and forth, as if he were verifying the information over and over again to be sure. By now I was ready to leave and spare myself the level of embarrassment that awaited me . . .

Until he spoke and said, "She scored low on one part of the test, but she got in."

Did I hear him correctly? Was I being admitted to a university?

Junisa was ecstatic. He smiled with pride and patted me on the back. I was floating around; I could not believe what was happening to me. We concluded the meeting and left. What a day it turned out to be!

Junisa decided that everyone should know what had happened, so he spread the word. Like him, I became a celebrity, only that my celebrity status lasted for a day, while his spark lasted the entire time we lived there.

I continued to work until everything was in place. It came to be that I was able to enroll, so I did. I had every intention of keeping my full-time position at work, so I elected to take six credits my first semester, because I did not want to overburden myself. I navigated these schedules for a while, but I was mentally unprepared to do both. While I was giving my all at work, I did not invest anywhere close to what I should have at school.

Like in Freetown and Italy, my interest in attaining an education plummeted. I was not doing well in my classes, nor was I aware of how to prioritize my schedules. Work had always been a priority to me, and so I did not know how to tailor it to meet the expectations of school life.

I decided to drop out after my first semester in the spring of 1998. I continued to work even more with the same clients. I also devoted myself to developing those skills I knew I needed in order to improve my overall self. I shielded myself from the rest of my friends, because I felt like I was incompetent.

My relationship with Ian's sister, who had become my best friend, had become frail, because she was busy managing her school load. Consequently, our time together dwindled. In the midst of it all, I had reconnected with my older cousin from Italy who had relocated to Maryland. She and I would often talk on the phone, and she became my confidant.

I didn't have much of a social life, except on weekends when I would socialize with some new friends who were not college students. Like me, they were in the workforce full time, so weekends were the time to party. They were unique in many ways. They were free-spirited and demonstrated an attitude of inclusion, which took me by surprise. Coming from Italy, where I had experienced a significant level of racism while in school (and almost everywhere else), I was shocked by their acceptance of me. These were all white young ladies, yet they acted as if we were from the same mother. I am not sure if they ever felt the level of hesitation I had toward them, because often, I didn't know how to act. I was accustomed to people my age running from me or refusing to socialize with me because of the color of my skin. Yes, even while I was in church. As a result, I did not know how to reciprocate their openness, which was something new to me.

As our friendship developed, I let my guard down, and we became sisters, a bond that has lasted to this day. My relationship with Ian's sister and the rest of his family also continued.

As I continued to work on improving myself after I ended my relationship with Ian, I was determined to erase what I had endured during our time together. However, I was thankful that we both had an opportunity to turn our lives around, and so I was determined to make the best out of mine.

I remained focused on me, devoting myself to my clients and

only those relationships that served a purpose in my life. Most of my coworkers, all of whom were Caucasian, became my family. I began to thrive. My life became drama-free. I started to rationalize that it was abnormal for a young woman such as myself to have deprived herself of attaining such level of peace in her life. I felt empowered!

During this time, I also traveled to Maryland to visit with my cousin. This escape also added to my overall development, as I began to form relationships with some of her friends who were much older than I. Their lives, it appeared, were drama-free, as well. I was hooked. I often visited, as I didn't have much to entertain myself with in my hometown, because the rest of my young-adult friends were busy with schoolwork. Moreover, I was not particularly interested in barhopping every weekend, which was the primary means of entertainment in our town.

During one of these visits, a friend of my cousin had introduced me to her lover's brother. I honestly wasn't all that interested in dating, because I was still reeling from my experience with Ian. With this in mind, I barely reciprocated his efforts at seducing me, but he persisted. His zeal I later attributed to our age difference. He was five years older than I and was a lot more mature than I was. It was perhaps his level of maturity that caused me to change my mind, as I eventually gave in, and we began to communicate by phone almost daily.

My friendship with him continued for a while before he came to visit me in Wisconsin. He had shared that he was separated from his wife and had two small boys. I was dumbfounded, but then realized that he was approaching thirty years of age, and so he must have lived a life that was different from mine. During this time, I had been committed to leading a drama-free life. Most importantly, I had not dated anyone who had children before, nor had I been involved with a married/separated man. I didn't know how to react to his revelation, and I kept my heart closed to all of it.

Up until then, my history with men had kept repeating itself. I was determined to seek an alternative. I deserved better than what I had experienced thus far. I was open and honest with him, so I shared my position. We continued to remain friends. I also kept up my regular visits to Maryland. During this time, he showered me with flowers, which he would send often. He communicated well with me and showed respect, which was something I had not had in my prior relationships. Thus, through his noble gestures, he won my heart, which eventually allowed for us to begin dating.

Yes, he was persistent.

As we continued to learn about each other, I began to learn things about him that were similar to what I had known from my previous relationships. Undoubtedly, he was a liar and a cheater. He disguised himself well—something he was able to do because we had a long-distance relationship.

I also came to find out that while he had moved on from his marriage, his wife was desperately attempting to save it. She called me once while he was visiting me to share some of her truths. Yes, my desire to lead a drama-free life was altering fast. I could not say or do much but listen to her. I allowed her to share what she felt I needed to know, and thanked her in the end.

Perché io sono sempre al centro dei problemi e perché devi vederci i segni prima che la mia vita cambi? (Why am I always in the middle of drama, and why can't I see the signs before my life changes?)

That day, I made up my mind to end my relationship with him. You guessed it: it didn't end at all. Instead, he wowed me even more by visiting me more frequently. He was by all accounts proving that he wanted to be with me and that he loved me. While I was conflicted, he was able to convince me that he was, in fact, through with his previous relationship. And so, we continued our relationship . . . until I became pregnant.

Things immediately changed. I realized that I had become an escape from the responsibility that he had not wanted to assume when his reaction to my pregnancy was for me to have an abortion. I then knew that it was not about love at all that made him so invested in me, but rather that he loved being "free"—free from those commitments that required him to be a man and a father. He enjoyed the single lifestyle, in which there weren't the same expectations as that of parenting and being a husband.

I was at a crossroads. I didn't know what to do, and so I confided in my cousin, who in turn told everyone what I had shared with her in secret. In the end, I succumbed to what other people felt was the "best thing for my life." My cousin had advised that I fly down to Maryland. There, she would assist me with locating an abortion clinic so I could have an abortion.

I did.

I made plans and headed to Maryland, and I stayed with my cousin and her roommates. When the time came, she drove me to the location and left me there for the procedure. I was alone. I truly don't remember how long I stayed at the clinic. Also, I don't remember the full details of the procedure or about my emotions that day.

After the procedure, my cousin and one of her roommates came to pick me up. On the drive home, I sat quietly in the backseat listening to my cousin detailing the events that led to the decision for me to have the abortion. Basically, she shared that my then-boyfriend had requested it. It was as if I was not in the car with them at all as she shared my private information so casually with her roommate. It made me sick to my stomach, but I continued to listen without saying a word as we made the drive back to their place.

I stayed with my cousin for a few more days before returning to Wisconsin. Upon my return, I resorted to my coping mechanism, which was work. I buried myself in my work, closing myself up to all else. I spent much of my time alone. It was then that I began to reflect on some of the miraculous events that had been happening to me, mainly through my dreams. Although I could not fully understand the meaning, I recognized that something different was happening in my life. During my relationship with Ian, I had dreamed on several occasions of events—visions that I had not adhered to entirely as I should have moving forward.

Because these dreams usually pertained to other people, I decided to start sharing some of my dreams with others. Two dreams in particular at the time had to do with my coworkers, one of whom was a newlywed desiring to have a baby. For reasons unknown to me, she was experiencing difficulty conceiving. I was only privy to this information by other coworkers to whom she had vented. They weren't gossiping about her, but instead were compassionate toward her situation. Out of the blue one day, I dreamt that she was going to have a baby girl. Yes, just like that.

When I returned to work, I shared my dream with her and others who knew of her desire. My coworker's reaction was one that suggested that I had lost my mind. Needless to say, it wasn't long after that she shared with all of us that she was pregnant with a little girl. When the time came, she gave birth to a beautiful baby girl, which was a gift that made all of us grateful.

My other dream involved another coworker who desired to have a baby boy. Well, needless to say, I dreamt that she was going to have a baby boy. Yes, her outcome was the same as the other. She gave birth to a baby boy, whom she named Jacob.

Through it all, I still didn't know what all of it meant, and so I did not fully understand what my role in all of it was, nor did I realize that having these dreams was a tremendous gift that I had. I was not limited to those two dreams, but continued to dream of many others, and the same goes for my life, as well.

During this time, I had decided to return to college and give it another try. It had been three years, to be exact, since I had first attempted to attain a college education. In the spring of 2001, I reenrolled in college and signed up for nine credits this time in my attempt to complete my degree.

I could immediately sense that I was different. My approach was different. Everything about school became a priority. I positioned myself to learn all that I could to ensure that I got good grades. Determined to succeed, I went to help sessions almost daily. On many occasions several times a day, I associated with other girls in my classes whom I knew were smart based on their grades. I humbled myself by asking for their guidance with what I needed to learn to succeed. My approach worked. In turn, I became inseparable with three of them, one of whom I am still friends with to this day.

I also had a good mentor at the writing lab whose teachings have stuck with me for most of my adult years. I also had a fabulous English teacher whose wisdom and compassion made a huge difference in my approach to endeavor until the end.

I decided to major in public relations and minor in journalism. This decision was a result of my fascination with Oprah Winfrey and the late Peter Jennings. The two had served as my TV mentors as I was learning English. I thought they were so proper that I needed to emulate everything about them. Therefore, I made up my mind on which career path I would blaze once I finished college.

Well, this plan changed once I decided to take a part-time job at a nursing home. There, I experienced things that no human being should be the subject of under any circumstances. As I watched my coworkers provide care for their patients, I felt disgusted in the way they would go about it. Everything about their care techniques lacked human dignity and compassion.

Being as affected as I was by what I saw, one day at school I inquired about a career path that would enable me to provide care for the elderly. I learned of three primary fields: psychology, sociology, and social work. As I began investigating the three, I gravitated more toward sociology, which is the study of the development, structure, and functioning of human society. It also focuses on the social problems and the overall well-being of a community. I knew I had found where I belonged.

I continued with my classes during that semester, and in the end, I had all As with a 4.0 GPA. By this time, I had requested a meeting with my advisor to relate that I wanted to change my major, which was something that didn't go over well with my English teacher. She thought the world of me. She believed I had potential in her field, so was naturally devastated. However, I knew in my heart what I needed to study so I could make a difference in the lives of the elderly. I became passionate about implementing a different approach to elderly care, so much so that I changed my major and began taking classes in my field. At the same time, I became passionate about criminal justice, as I also desired to be an immigration attorney.

I remained focused in school, and my efforts to attain good grades continued, which resulted in me earning between a 3.5 and a 4.0 GPA nearly every semester. I made the dean's list on many occasions up until my last semester in December of 2003. I had devoted two and a half years to taking between eighteen to twenty-one credits, as well as attending summer school, and so I graduated from a four-year university in two and a half years with a bachelor's in sociology and a minor in criminal justice. I had devoted myself to school while still working full time, as I couldn't let my clients down.

Most importantly, I knew I needed to conquer something more for myself, mainly because I also had someone that was going to become dependent on me.

I had reconciled with my ex from Maryland, who once again was resolute in not letting me go. We dated briefly, but this time things weren't the same as they had been. I was alert. I had gained a sense of self. I knew my potential, and so I did not settle for less, as far as he was concerned. As we continued to date, I became pregnant again. His response was the same as before, only this time he asked, "When are we going to take care of the problem?" While he had included me in the decision, he was still telling me to have an abortion.

I stood my ground and decided that I wasn't going to abort my child. I did not share my news with anyone, as I did not want anyone's influence on my decision this time around. With my baby in my belly, I walked the stage on the day of graduation and received my diploma. I had graduated with honors—magna cum laude, to be exact—and with a 3.622 GPA. I had no one in the crowd except for the family of one of my friends, as she, too, graduated that same day. They shook the bell that they had brought to honor her on my behalf as I walked up the stage with my belly hidden under my gown. All the while, I was thinking to myself that I was not alone. Not only had I made myself proud, but someday my baby girl would be, as well.

After graduation, I continued to work at the same place while I anticipated the arrival of my girl. My friendship with most of the women at work was in full swing. They supported me throughout my pregnancy and even hosted a baby shower on my behalf.

My dear friend from Maryland who in the end became my sister was also supportive of me. She had come to visit with me the weekend of March 26, 2004. We spent the entire weekend out and about doing activities—more than I had ever done since becoming pregnant. I could hardly move, as I had gained more than seventy pounds at that point in my pregnancy. My feet were swollen more than usual that weekend, but I didn't want to let her down, so I engaged in all of what she wanted to do.

Unbeknownst to the both of us, that Sunday evening after I had returned from taking her to the airport, my baby girl was ready to make her arrival into the world! Mind you, though, she had several more weeks to go. With this in mind, I did not understand what was happening when I felt fluid gush down my legs. I immediately called the after-hours number for my OB/GYN, who advised that I call 911.

Okay, I was naïve in all of it, and so I did call 911, and they instructed that they were going to send an ambulance to my home. I informed them that I was not hurting and that I could make it to the hospital, which was only a few minutes away from my apartment. I don't remember how I convinced the operator, but I did, and I drove myself to the ER that night. Upon my arrival, I called my supervisor to share that I was at the ER, but that I would make it into work afterward. I was scheduled to work at 10 p.m.

After my evaluation at the ER, they informed me that I was in labor and that I would have to be transported to another town, as the baby was going to be premature. Again, I had no clue what was happening. I was a first-time mother. I was alone, with no one who could share their experiences or who at least had experienced what I now had to face.

I kept calm and followed all of their recommendations. The entire team was friendly and professional. After they ensured that the baby was safe, I was transported to another hospital by ambulance. During the ride there, the ambulance workers weren't so friendly, as they shared that I was crazy for driving myself to the hospital when I went into labor. I told them that I didn't know what was happening to me, as the baby had not been due for several more weeks. They understood my position, and it then became a gracious ride. Along with the EMT workers, the hospital sent along a maternity nurse who was responsible for my and my baby's overall health until our arrival. We arrived safely.

By now we had gone into March 29, 2004. The doctors at the other hospital got us situated and continued to monitor our health. I remember an intern who was shadowing a seasoned doctor. Both of them were males. I was a bit shy, as my regular OB/GYN was a female. She had been scheduled to deliver my baby. However, now here I was with two men who were going to assist in my delivery. I was particularly embarrassed, as I believed that the young doctor was not even old enough (in my estimation) to be in the room and see my naked parts. But what could I have done?

My Camilla had decided to make her grand entrance, contrary to what the doctors had told me. They had advised that I would be in labor for most of the day and that I probably wouldn't give birth until late the next evening. They weren't even prepared for her arrival, as everything happened so fast. Suffice to say, it was a surprise to both doctors and a nurse when I pushed my call button to suggest that something was wrong. My pain had intensified. I now wanted the epidural that I had refused when I signed my intake forms. Nevertheless, it could not be given to me, as the baby was on her way.

In the early hours of March 29, 2004, at 4:29 a.m., Camilla graced us with her presence. I was not able to hold her right away, as she was a preemie and they needed to rush her off into an incubator. A few hours later, I had the privilege of cradling her in my arms. She stole my heart, and our relationship began.

Shortly after that, my manager and assistant manager arrived at the hospital to see the new member of our family. Their eyes were full of joy. They took turns holding her so tenderly that I knew these ladies were a blessing to me.

While Camilla stayed in the neonatal unit, I was in my room. I would visit with her during the timeframe I had for nursing her. Just as I had been alone in the delivery room, so I was in the bedroom, where I stayed for a couple more days before my discharge.

All of my other close friends were out of town. Thankfully, though, Ian's sister was able to free up some time, so she came to pick me up from the hospital and was very instrumental in helping me during those first few weeks as a new mother. Because Camilla was premature, I had to leave her in the hospital so she could be monitored until she could breathe on her own. She was hooked up to several machines and had a tube inserted in her little nose. I was restless knowing that I had to leave her alone.

Faced with the hospital's order of leaving Camilla behind, I inquired about staying at the Ronald McDonald House that was minutes away from the hospital—a discovery that came about through one of the nurses in the neonatal unit who took care of Camilla. She was very good to Camilla and me. She would teach me how to encourage Camilla to latch on to my nipples, as she had not yet developed those skills because she was a preemie. Often, this nurse realized how unfamiliar I was with all things associated with motherhood, and so she would serve as a mentor during those times.

I stayed at the Ronald McDonald House for about a week, making scheduled visits to breastfeed Camilla and spending time with her. Those moments were the hardest because our time together was limited, as she needed to be back in the incubator at a set time. It was a difficult time. We endured every bit of it, though.

One afternoon, I came home to my apartment to wash clothes when I received a call from our nurse, who informed me that

Camilla would be discharged within the next few days. To my surprise, Camilla had done well, the nurse explained, and so there was no need for her to continue to stay there. I breathed a sigh of relief. I was thrilled and thankful at the same time.

The nurse told me everything I needed to have in place, what infant car seat I should bring to the hospital, and so forth. I immediately called my best pal, Ian's sister. She made arrangements on her end and was there with me to bring Camilla home at the end of that very same week.

We took lots of pictures of Camilla that day. We dressed her like a princess and held her like she was a piece of fine, expensive china. She was a treasure!

Shortly after arriving home from the hospital, I had an emergency where Camilla stopped breathing. It was a miracle that I was able to resuscitate her by patting her on the back like I had learned to do while in Freetown. Yes, everything required a pat on the back to bring you back to life from whatever obstruction had taken place. It turned out that Camilla had not fully developed her breathing, and so she was admitted into the hospital for a few more days until she stabilized. It was a blessing, however, because she's remained a healthy child since then.

When things settled for Camilla and me, my coworker, manager, and assistant manager took turns supporting me with babysitting so I could continue to work. In the meantime, I knew I could not burden them as much as I was. With this in mind, I reached out to my aunt and cousins, who had moved to Georgia by then. I inquired about visiting with them, as I needed a more realistic plan for both Camilla and me. They welcomed my request, and so Camilla and I visited Georgia for the first time.

Our visit went well. Camilla bonded with my younger cousin and fell in love with my older cousin's son, who was about two years older than she. I was grateful for this, because I had been considering moving there. Subsequently, we revisited Georgia several more times before I finally decided on relocating.

It was during one of our visits that my older cousin introduced me to a friend of hers. Yes, it was to be another love connection. By all accounts, this time, he seemed to be a seasoned man with a definite understanding of his desires and expectations. He was much older than I and had two young children in Sierra Leone. He seemed ideal.

I'd now come to form a sense of self, mainly because I needed to shelter Camilla from all I had allowed previously in my life. I had laid out a perfect plan of what my next relationship should entail, so this man and I began to talk, mainly via telephone. I asked what I thought were the right questions to assess his intentions. He passed with flying colors, and so it came to be that we started to date. Like with my daughter's father, our relationship was a long-distance one, as I still resided in Wisconsin at the time.

It was during the same visit that I was introduced to him that I also asked my younger cousin, whom Camilla had grown attached to, if she would assist me by keeping Camilla for me for a while as I prepared to move to Georgia permanently. She agreed. Also, I needed to seek permission from her mother, who was, by all accounts, partly a decision-maker on her behalf. I did, and she, too, agreed.

After Camilla and I returned to Wisconsin, I focused on getting ready for our separation. Although it was going to be for a short period—six months to be exact—it was one of the hardest decisions I have ever had to make. I began to think of my mother and how she must have felt when she gave my siblings and me to her mother to raise, and my grandmother, who gave my sister and me to our fathers. I could not fathom their despair.

I had one of the most unusual feelings I had ever felt. I was broken and conflicted at the same time knowing that I could not adequately care for Camilla, as I did not have the proper support system in place, just like my mother and grandmother: different times in our lives, but same outcome. Camilla was bouncing from home to home as my coworkers took turns babysitting her while I worked. Through my hurting, I knew she deserved better, and so that served as my biggest motivation for following through with letting her go.

The time came to take Camilla to Georgia, which seemed sudden. She had just celebrated her first birthday. In the interim of all of my brokenness, something happened that I was not expecting: my long-distance boyfriend asked for my hand in marriage. I was a bit surprised, but without hesitation, I accepted. I was now a single mother. Life had granted me a different outcome from what I had initially desired. Thus, I believed his proposal came at the right time.

I believed the life I had once envisioned for myself, which was to not have a child out of wedlock, was somehow going to be possible if I were to become a married woman. Growing up, I never wanted to have a child out of wedlock. I dreamt of having a nuclear family like that of my uncle's.

Consequently, when my boyfriend proposed, I started to fantasize about having my family unit. My childhood dream was now going to become a reality! We got married less than six months after our initial introduction. It was an intimate ceremony, with my aunt serving as our witness with Camilla in her arms. We got married at the courthouse, and our reception was at a low-key Jamaican restaurant with just the four of us.

We did not have a honeymoon, as I needed to return to Wisconsin to continue with my planning. I could not begin to describe how I felt. I now had to leave Camilla behind, as well as my new husband, for that matter. It was devastating, because I knew she was my responsibility. Camilla had not asked to be born, and so I felt that I was letting her down. I cried. I could not feel my heartbeat as I hugged her goodbye. I refused to let her come along for the ride to the airport, because I hoped to spare her of any recollection of that day. Through it all, I was grateful that she had come to love my cousin. The two of them were bonding so effortlessly, which eased my anguish to a certain degree.

I returned to Wisconsin and continued to work long hours. I now needed to provide not only for myself and my family back home, but Camilla, as well, because even though she was living with my cousin, I was financially responsible for her upkeep. My husband did pay for daycare from time to time. I also wanted to make sure that I had enough money to allow me to visit with her, which I was able to do twice before my final move.

My focus was on saving as much as I could. I thank God that my clients continued to need me, which enabled me to accomplish all that I needed to accomplish. Furthermore, six months after our separation, I was finally able to make plans for my relocation to Georgia.

As I began to say my final goodbyes to most of my friends in Wisconsin, I felt a tremendous loss. I had come to form a community with these people, many of whom are still living there. I was grateful for all of their support and dedication. They had sacrificed a lot on my behalf, and continued in their efforts when Camilla came along. I had come to treasure all of these friendships, because every one of them served a purpose in my life. I was thankful for my work family, whose dedication was unmatched by many that I have come to experience thus far in my life. Also, my relationship with Ian was undoubtedly a humbling experience that allowed me to gain wisdom and credibility about my truth, helping to shape the woman that I became. Grateful for my history in Wisconsin, I counted all of my blessings as I repositioned myself for what would be my final days there.

A few days before I was to leave permanently, my husband flew up to help with getting things ready for my move. He played a big part in getting everything together, so I was able to leave as planned. That weekend, we packed my remaining items—mostly clothes, as I had sold everything else—and we made the fifteen-hour drive to Georgia, stopping only a few times.

There is no logical explanation that I can provide you as to how this chapter of my life ended as it did, except that I do believe that my steps were ordered way before I ventured on navigating these territories.

Chapter Four

Georgia

We started our lives in Georgia in 2005. By all means, things were going great for us. I bonded with my cousins, which was nice because I had not had an opportunity to do so when we lived in Italy. Furthermore, Camilla was thriving in her new environment. She continued to attend the daycare where my cousin worked, so they were able to maintain their relationship. Moreover, we lived with my husband's friend, where my husband had been staying, and he was exceptionally gracious enough to allow us all to stay with him for a period of about six months. This living arrangement continued to provide stability for us, because in the meantime we were waiting for a builder to finish building the townhome I had purchased.

Life for us in Georgia began as planned. I had my nuclear family. I was a married woman. My daughter had a father. All that I lacked growing up was now in my reach. I felt empowered.

Once we were finally able to move into our new home, everything fell into place. My husband worked as a delivery driver for a medical-equipment company while I continued to work in social services as a certified nursing assistant. I considered our new beginning a tremendous blessing.

I continued to try my hardest to ensure we maintained what I had always desired. I worked seven days a week, as my husband's job was somewhat inconsistent. With what my husband was earning at the time, it would have been impossible for us to make ends meet if I had just worked forty hours a week at ten dollars per hour. By the way, he earned the same pay rate as me.

We managed like this for a while, but I was hopeful that he would become eager to find a job that was more feasible to meeting our financial needs. This was not the case, and things got complicated. It turned out that my husband did not share my enthusiasm for working hard and was content at being basic. Subsequently, our marriage began to deteriorate, and we began to argue a lot because I had expressed that he needed to find another job with better earnings, which in turn would offer us financial stability. Furthermore, I was exhausted from working seven days a week and driving forty-five minutes each way every day. He, on the other hand, worked part-time on most occasions, as his company would call on him only when he was needed. On some occasions, he did not work at all.

This hurdle went on for some time, but I remained patient, because Camilla needed stability. I valued that she had a father. With my daughter's well-being in mind, I again sacrificed myself and endured for three long years in the same position. It came to the point where he refused to work at all, because he said that complications with his back prevented him from working. Thus, I became responsible for our household income while he stayed home. He defended his lack of enthusiasm for work by saying that he was caring for Camilla while I was at work.

By now, I was ready to forfeit the perfect image that I had been presenting on the outside. I gave him an ultimatum, which in essence was "You find a job or leave." He refused to do either. Fed up, I packed a few things for Camilla and myself, and moved out of the home I had purchased on my own. I left him at our house. I said "our house" because he was my husband, and I acknowledged him in everything, as we had become one.

Camilla and I moved in with a woman with whom I had formed a very close friendship. She was a friend of my younger cousin, and I got along very well with her. She welcomed us with open arms. She had a son who was a bit younger than Camilla.

We all shared a one-bedroom apartment for a while. Eventually, my husband realized that I was not returning home, so he called me one day to inform me that he was going to move out.

The truth is, this decision did not happen willingly. I had stopped paying most of the bills, because my financial responsibilities were greater than what I earned. Overwhelmed by all of my financial obligations, I let the home go into foreclosure. He had no choice but to move out, so Camilla and I were able to return home after that. By now, though, I could not afford to continue living there, as we were so far behind on the mortgage, which caused my first home to go into foreclosure. I had to file for bankruptcy. We practically lost everything.

Thankfully, the bank allowed me time to make other living arrangements when I shared that I had a young daughter and asked them for mercy. The time came when we were scheduled to leave. Something happened the day of our move that left me baffled. The mediator that came to do a walkthrough and to whom I was handing over the key gave me a check for a thousand dollars to help with our move. I was speechless. I expressed my gratitude, and when all was said and done, that chapter of our lives ended.

Ironically, this situation did not break me, because all of the challenges I encountered before had prepared me to handle where life had placed Camilla and me. I dealt with this situation with grace.

By now I was a newly hired program manager for a company that managed group homes for individuals with cerebral palsy, traumatic brain injuries, and mental disabilities. My base salary was low, about thirty-seven thousand dollars a year. I was now a single mother, and I still had the financial responsibility of my family back home. I was concerned, but I knew it was a step up from being a CNA. Furthermore, I could now put my degree to work.

I worked hard. I became good at what I was expected to do. I associated with a couple of my colleagues who'd made a name for themselves. Also, I made sure that I positioned myself to learn from my direct supervisor, who was ahead of everyone as it related to compliance and budgetary outcomes. The head of management greatly valued these accomplishments. Recognizing the qualities that my employer valued, I asked if he could mentor me, as I wanted to learn these skills to succeed. He agreed.

I started to shadow with him, and he taught me a lot. I learned everything I could from him. I was thriving. My homes gained recognition for zero citations after the mandated audits by the state. Also, I kept a low budget while minimizing overtime hours. My team and I were able to use less of our allocated annual budget, which caused our team to soar. We were so successful that staff members from other groups would request to join my team—something that I was not always fond of, but I accepted those staff members I knew I could mentor so they could earn an opportunity to gain leadership positions, as well—a goal I was able to attain as a regional manager.

Within a year of being employed as a program manager, the regional-director position became available. I applied for it, along with several seasoned program managers. With this new opportunity came trials and tribulations, meaning not everyone thought I was qualified to apply for such a position. After all, I had only gained a year's worth of experience with this particular company, and for most of my working years I had held positions that weren't similar to this one. Most importantly, I would be the youngest in the company to assume such a position. My peers were determined to prove that I was unqualified.

Undeterred by their opinions of me, I remained focused. I went through the rigorous process of updating my résumé, attending the interview, and completing the regional director's questionnaire that we were given to complete—something I take no credit for having accomplished on my own. My direct supervisor believed in my potential, so he was the one who suggested that I apply for the position. He helped me significantly during the process, as well, and in the end, I got the position. I became a regional director responsible for a total of twelve group homes and all the staff members working in those homes in the regions. I was scattered all over

Georgia. Yes, it was a new challenge, but one I felt prepared to assume.

I repositioned myself to accept a more significant workload than I had ever imagined. Thankfully, everything started going well for my team and me. I made sure to pass on to my staff members and other interdisciplinary team members what Mamma and Joe had contributed to my life. I made it a point to inspire everyone to reach their full potential, regardless of what position he or she held with the company. I made sure I encouraged all of them to regard me as a team member, not as a director/supervisor, which was most important to me.

To gain their trust and cooperation, I made it a point to visit every home weekly, which was far from the mandated requirement of once monthly. Also, many staff members were much older than I, so my goal was to value their contributions, as some had been working there for years before my arrival. I remained humble, and my humility contributed to most of our successes.

A huge turnaround came to be regarding our clients. They were reaching their goals and had become interested in activities that they previously would not have been willing to participate in. Moreover, other interdisciplinary teams began to recognize our accomplishments, so the executive director acknowledged our team on many occasions during meetings and sometimes by sending out a mass email to the entire company. We worked well as a team. Most importantly, we respected one another.

As I juggled my position as a regional director, I also was orchestrating a move to a different city, as I wanted to move to a town that would afford Camilla a better education. I knew the schools close to where we resided weren't performing well, because they had very low test scores. Camilla had been identified as a gifted student while in pre-K, so I knew that I needed to foster her potential. I inquired with my coworkers and supervisor about cities with schools that had better academic standards. I was made aware of three towns, which I familiarized myself with before making a decision. I eventually decided on the one where we still reside to this day.

Shortly after deciding on the town, we moved into a townhome, which I agreed to do a lease-purchase agreement on for a couple of years. By now, we had become stable. Camilla began elementary school as a gifted student. She made several friends and joined Girl Scouts. Her little life was busy, and so was mine.

I continued in my position. My team and I continued to excel. We were thriving, and we made a name for ourselves. Our success was so apparent that I was asked to assume the responsibility of another house, which raised my caseload to thirteen homes. This was a direct request from the executive director. I obliged, but not before I negotiated my salary. I knew what I was worth to the company.

With this increase, it came to be that my salary was fifty thousand dollars per year, which was thousands of dollars fewer than what I had proposed for the additional caseload. I was saving the company millions of dollars annually, and I knew how much my region brought in. In the end, I settled, as this, too, was a step up from where I had been.

With thirteen group homes now under my belt, we continued to be the best team of the other two regions by all accounts. Yet having accomplished what I had within a relatively short period of time, my immediate supervisor became threatened by my success. He began making my work life miserable. He had a biased attitude toward me that caused me to feel a lot of tension.

He was the only associate director over all four regional directors, which made him our only immediate supervisor. Although I was uncomfortable with all of his harassment, I could not change supervisors. I endured his many baseless accusations to the point that it became obvious he was looking to get rid of me. There had been several email exchanges and meetings with the executive director, because he had written me up on baseless accusations. I would defend my position and challenge him by going directly to the executive director (something that no one else ever did), as I knew I was doing my job effectively and so was my team.

He did not succeed at his first attempts, until he brought up another baseless claim about an error regarding medication administration. Well, I was not a registered nurse (RN) and was not directly responsible for overseeing the overall management of any clients' medications. It was the responsibility of the RN assigned to my region. Nevertheless, he attempted to place me on a performance-improvement plan (PIP) for this error relating to one of my homes. Interestingly, he bypassed all of the initial steps regarding disciplinary action and opted for the very last one, a PIP.

I received an email from him summoning me to a meeting. He had copied in the human-resources (HR) director. It didn't take long for me to conclude that he had another accusation against me. I was not concerned at all, as I had been the one to write-up the error and emailed everyone who needed to know about it. I came prepared.

As our meeting convened, he could barely get his words out because he stuttered, but also because he was extremely nervous. I kept my cool and listened to his report. After he had finished, I presented my initial email and argued my case by stating that I was not the RN, but I still had caught the error that the nurse had missed. I also shared that I had brought the error to everyone's attention. I further stated that his decision to put me on a PIP was unjustified. Confident that I had followed protocol and done what was right, I refused to sign his write-up.

The HR director did not say a word during our exchange. Rather, she sat as a witness, something that I thought very strange.

After I presented my case, I got up and left, and upon arriving home, I sent out my resignation letter to the entire company. The following is a copy:

October 25, 2012

Hello everyone,

> *Please be advised that I have decided to resign my position as regional director of community living services for the South Region effective today. I thank all of you for your*

support, dedication, and service to the individuals we serve. I wish you all success in your continued roles as members of the South Region family.

For those of you that I directly worked with, I thank you from the bottom of my heart for your contributions to my success during my years of service. The South Region succeeded because of your tireless efforts, compassion, and your understanding of who the beneficiaries are.

Please never cease to believe that your actions impact their lives. I will miss you. However, please know that you will always be a part of my professional growth, as I am taking all that I have learned, good or bad, to help my continued achievements as I transition into the new endeavor that God has destined for me.

Many blessings to you!

I close with the words of Abraham Lincoln . . .

"I am not bound to win, but I am bound to be true. I am not bound to success, but I am bound to live by the light that I have. I must stand with anybody that stands right, and stand with him while he is right, and part with him when he goes wrong."

Best,
Laura Jaka

Interestingly, here again, I failed to adhere to the inner voice that had been prompting me to leave before it was time for our meeting. I had the most unsettling feeling all that day while I was at the office, and my stomach was in knots. I stayed, as I believed I needed to confront whatever my supervisor had brought against me for what would be his third attempt.

Before this day, I had been warned by another regional director who had experienced the same level of harassment from him as he, too, was thriving at some point in his position, but his success was often met with the same kind of hostility as mine. Frustrated with all I had been through with him, I was determined to see and hear whatever it was.

It became apparent that I was unique in the sense that I could dream and sense events that were about to happen to me—and others, for that matter—but I was not paying attention to any of it at the time. However, my resignation was a decision I felt proud of, because I could not let my supervisor oppress me by intimidating me with his methods. I did not give him the power that he wanted over me. I had no reason to subject myself to his bullying, and I needed to decide for myself how my story would end with this company. Nevertheless, I am not sure if I handled this situation as I should have, but I knew I had developed a level of trust in God's ability to make a way, regardless of my failure to adhere, that I was certain that He would see me through to the next best thing.

I had been practicing a stronger praying habit, so my faith was a million times more developed than it was in my years in Charlotte and Wisconsin. Before moving to Georgia, I had no recollection of ever having an intimate relationship with God, even though I attended church. My great-grandfather, great-grandmother, and grandmother baptized me as a child. My father ensured that I received confirmation before his return home, and I went to confession almost weekly, because it was a requirement at school while I lived in Italy. But, it took a tremendous amount of pain, trials, and tribulations—and even several incidents that would have cost me my life or my freedom—to get me to adhere to God's many attempts to walk side by side with me. With many financial obligations and as a single mother, my alternative after my resignation was to ensure my faith was at the forefront of my vision.

I went home and began searching for employment, and I eventually landed a job working with the State. I worked primarily in a halfway house supervising adults who'd committed severe crimes, including murder, and who'd spent most of their lives in prison. These residents, which was what we called them, were now in rehabilitation in the halfway house before making their full return into the community. It was very frightening, but I had become hooked on the belief that, unless the Lord guides the city, the watchman stays awake in vain (Psalm 127:1, ESV). This verse became my daily prayer when I worked at night at what was, by all accounts, a dangerous job.

I continued to look for additional work, as I needed an extra income to be able to meet all of my financial obligations. I was blessed with another position where I worked as a developmental disability professional (DDP). In essence, I was responsible for compliance and the overall health and safety of my employer's clients and the management of their staff members. My responsibilities with this employer were somewhat similar to those of when I worked as a program manager.

This particular employer had several homes in different cities that I would visit either weekly or monthly, depending. I was also able to add several more clients for whom I worked as a DDP, as well. I would drive about a thousand miles per week, or maybe even more, because I needed to visit all of their sites as part of my job requirement.

Under my supervision, the employers for whom I worked as a DDP began to thrive. I had learned from my previous employer the importance of maintaining a citation-free home, so I was determined that they, too, would succeed—a goal I was able to achieve for several of them. I juggled three jobs as a DDP and still held my position with the State for years.

Mentally and physically, I was exhausted. Camilla was again at the mercy of my friends who God had placed in our path. Their support of us was endless.

Then there came a time when I became so emotionally drained. My employers' expectations of me were widening. I became aware that I was stretching myself too thin. My ability began to falter. Nevertheless, I would have persevered, but I became discouraged, as all of my employers were primarily thinking of themselves and not the clients or staff members, who were the reasons they had businesses in the first place. It seemed that all of my employers were obsessed with material possessions and leading a lavish lifestyle.

Their degree of greed was one I had not experienced before. I felt hurt for my clients and the staff members. Also, my stomach could not digest what I was privy to. The attitudes of these employers brought back those feelings I had when I worked in the nursing home, which prompted me to work in social services. I had vowed to be an advocate. These employers had hired me to be an advocate for the clients and staff, so I could not look the other way.

I shared my concerns when it was appropriate for me to do so, and I was diplomatic in my response to their lack of consideration for the people affording them the many blessings they had through God's giving. I made it a point to share my opinion often, because change was needed. I mean, these clients lived beyond what they should have had. The staff members were being paid less than what I believed was appropriate for the work they did. There's no way that anyone would be eager to give their fullest to both the clients, who required a lot, and to the employer while being paid seven or eight dollars per hour.

Eventually, I shared what I knew the clients needed based on my conversations with both the staff members and the clients. These were minor requests, including things such as advanced technology and activities that would promote a person-centered approach to living.

Also, I recommended that my employers increase their hourly/annual pay to attract qualified staff members and to help minimize the level of staff turnover. My suggestions were unwelcomed and met with hostility and excuses. Nevertheless, I knew what I was trying to accomplish on their behalf, but their greed would not afford them the level of dignity that both the staff and clients deserved.

I felt discouraged, as my position was to oversee the overall operation of their facilities, which meant that my recommendations should have mattered. Moreover, I knew that the clients were being funded adequately by the State, and thus their needs should've been of priority.

Another issue that bothered me was that these employers would not pay their staff members on a regular basis (including me). Instead, they would cite that they weren't getting paid by the State promptly, which I knew was untrue.

Well, you can probably guess what became of me after challenging my employers: I ended up being terminated by two of my employers, while the third suggested that her budget was low, and so she needed to put me on a break for a while, but with a promise that I would be called back into work a few weeks later. Meanwhile, I had just resigned from my position with the State in order to free up some time for my job as a DDP, as I was working with three different agencies and their expectations of me had mounted. Having been terminated by two of my employers and being placed on leave by another, I once again became jobless, going from having four jobs to zero. Now I was at a place of mercy.

I did what I had learned to do: I prayed and depended on God. Even though nothing happened for a while, I persevered and kept my situation to myself, until one day when I decided to share with a colleague who worked for the same employer who had placed me on leave. I told her what had transpired and that I had not been back to work. She suggested that I file for unemployment, which I did, since it had been several months and I had not been called to return. I was approved for unemployment for the allocated duration that the government allowed.

By now, I had purchased another home. Unfortunately, it happened again that Camilla and I were almost homeless, as I was very behind on the mortgage payments and could barely make ends meet during this time. There were times when some of our utilities were cut off. We ate plain cooked rice with butter for a very long time and managed with whatever else we could find. We drove our old car, which was on its last legs, that I had been able to purchase for about $2,500. The entire neighborhood knew when we were leaving and coming home because of the smoke that our car let out once the engine was turned on.

However, I had developed what I needed most out of life: faith!

I now had a stronger relationship with God. I prayed without ceasing. It was during my test that I had a dream that I should write a letter to the mortgage company and share my current situation. By now, I had learned from my days in Wisconsin, particularly with my relationship with Ian and my experience with my associate executive director, to adhere to every message in my dreams or that inner voice of mine. When I got up, I wrote the letter to my mortgage company explaining that I had lost my job. It was brief and straight to the point.

Up until this time, I had been current on my mortgage and at times paid more than my regular payment. But, my history of paying on time or more than what was required of me did not solidify that my home would not go into foreclosure. I was hopeful, however, because I knew that whenever God speaks, He has a solution at hand.

Shortly after I sent out the letter, I got a call from the person handling my file. She needed additional information from me. I provided everything she requested, and not long after that, I received a letter in the mail. In it, I was advised that my mortgage was going to be reduced to $550 per month for a period of twelve months. The mortgage company had granted me a modification! Initially, my mortgage had been about $2,300 monthly.

There was a stipulation in place that I needed first to pay about ten thousand dollars of back payments on my mortgage in order for the modification to take effect. Well, I didn't have that amount of money.

I reached out to my cousin in California and requested to borrow some money. He could only afford to loan me one thousand dollars. I next called Ian's sister, my dearest friend at the time, and asked the same of her. Through God's divine intervention, she agreed to loan me the money. In about a week, I was able to pay the ten thousand dollars, preventing our home from being sold at a scheduled auction the following week.

When I received the final modification documents in the mail, I fell flat to the floor, face forward, thanking God and crying uncontrollably. I then called my cousin in California and Ian's sister to share God's miracle and grace toward Camilla and me, as they were the only people who became aware of where life had landed for us. Interestingly, I had not shared with them about me having to write the letter, because I had begun to learn not to share some messages from God until He provided the outcome. Also, I did not share with other relatives and close friends what we had been enduring, mainly because I didn't want to bother anyone with our problems.

Instead, I remember being so confident while stepping out and associating myself with others. I would dress so prestigiously and walk in a room as if I lacked nothing. Everything about my outside appearance at that time gave the impression that I was a woman who had it all together. Funnily, this was also the time that many people thought that I was a millionaire. I had no idea what prompted them to arrive at such an assumption of me. Perhaps it was already evident to them what God was about to do in my life. But, unbeknownst to them, I was crying my eyes out while rationally negotiating with God. I engaged in full-fledged conversations with Him, as I needed to know where I had gone wrong. It was interesting, to say the least.

It was also during this time that I started my own company, Wellington Place of Serenity (WPS), which I named after my beloved grandmother. Naturally, it had to be in social services. Wellington Place of Serenity is a private home-care company that provides skilled nursing, personal care, and companion-sitter services to clients in their homes or in a community setting. We offer one-on-one services to clients who need additional support with their activities of daily living.

As with many new businesses, mine was slow. Absolutely nothing was happening for me. We lived on my unemployment check, which I was grateful for, because it kept us afloat. I continued to pray and fast. I was devoted to my relationship with God, as I knew He was the only one who could change our situation. I began to speak casually with him more than the formal method of praying. I would ask questions that I thought would help me better understand the places He had brought me. I was curious to know what He was expecting of me and how I needed to go about following His directives. I earnestly sought answers from Him, because I knew He needed something from me.

Being the faithful Father that He is, He answered me in my dreams, many of which I could not interpret. I resorted to communicating and praying even more. We continued like this for a while as doors began to open. I had asked several things of Him. One in particular was, as a gift for my birthday that following year, that He give me a client so WPS could finally take root.

Well, He honored my request. Camilla and I were in New Jersey for Ian's sister's birthday party. She had invited me to celebrate my birthday with her, as our birthdays are only a week apart. There was not much celebration on my part, because I had a million other things taking my attention at that time. Nevertheless, I understood that she was trying to support me as a friend.

While we were visiting, we went to the grocery store to purchase items for the party. I distinctly remember our visit to the store and being embarrassed beyond words, repeatedly apologizing because I was not able to contribute a dime to all of the items she was purchasing. I felt as though I were useless. Being my friend, she was understanding about my position and showed empathy toward me.

At the end of our shopping, as we were putting the groceries in the trunk of her car, I got a call on my cell phone. On the other line was the admission's director from a facility where a man had taken me after a network event. He was the angel that God had positioned me to meet at that network event, because he and that facility became the vessels that have continued to overflow five-plus years after our initial encounter.

The voice said, "Laura!" I answered very quietly. The admission's director continued, "I have the daughter of a resident with me who is going to need your services starting on February 2."

Overwhelmed, I could hardly contain my excitement—so much

so that the daughter could barely understand my responses to all of the questions she asked me. I ended the conversation by stating that I had a bad connection and asking to call her back shortly.

Lo and behold, God had granted me my birthday wish! Based on our initial conversation, our first client would be starting on the day of my birthday, and WPS would take root. Good God Almighty!

I shared with my friend what had happened, and we praised God for His loving kindness. After I gained my composure, I followed up with the client's daughter to gather all of the relevant information about the client and arranged for proper coverage on his behalf before my return to Georgia. The feeling of excitement continued, and I could not contain myself the days following the call. I was eager to return to Georgia.

Immediately following my return, I visited the facility to meet him and learn a bit more about him before we accepted him as a formal client. Our meeting went well. He was friendly and very polite. Born and raised in Georgia, he had a Southern accent that kept me drawn to his every word. He was soft-spoken but very assertive. He was funny, too! He made it a point to tell me after our meeting that the caregiver whom I was sending him should be the representation of me. I agreed.

Then came the day: February 2. I took the staff along to meet him and his daughter at the facility. We interacted briefly before finally beginning our official business. We were going to serve him twelve hours per day, seven days a week. This event began the success of WPS.

Admitting my first client sparked a burning desire within me to gain more. I tailored my schedule to allow me to work a few days with him and also attend network meetings endlessly. I also pursued several marketing opportunities, as I wanted to expose WPS as much as I could. We were able to admit a few more clients from the facility where we had been, which kept us rolling, as nothing was materializing from all of my marketing efforts.

For the first year of WPS, the company's gross annual income was about $48,000. I was grateful. Nonetheless, my enthusiasm did not resonate well with an accounting firm that a client's friend had recommended I use. One of the partners turned down my request for them to take over my company's accounting, though he was very polite about it. He shared that he had turned me down because he did not want me to pay out an unnecessary amount of money to his firm, as my company had only generated that amount. He then referred me to a colleague of his that managed smaller accounts such as mine.

I set up my first meeting with his referral, and she took WPS on. What was fascinating about the first client and the one who referred me to his accounting friend was that they weren't only going to be clients of mine, but that through their connections, I would encounter some crucial people who would help me with finishing the remaining requirements of operating a business. While the company only earned $48,000 in its first year, the connections I was able to make were incomparable.

It turns out that I did not have a full understanding of how to run a business with all of its components. I had learned management skills and was sure of my ability to manage. My previous employers had people in place responsible for each aspect of the operation of their businesses. Thus, when I opened mine, I was unfamiliar with other essential requirements for each department and its regulations. Through these connections, I was set up with a payroll company, which in turn helped to set up my company with the Georgia Department of Labor, Georgia Department of Revenue, Internal Revenue Service, and other compliance agencies that I needed. My accounting firm was also instrumental in all of the financial aspects of running my business.

When it was all said and done, I was thankful that God had secretly positioned these people to guide me through. WPS was now in full swing!

I continued with my marketing strategy and hosted several events at different senior-living communities. Little did I know at the time that the facility where we had gotten our first clients would be where our abundance of blessings would flow. We had done a tremendous job with the first few clients, so much so that everyone in the facility began to refer us to clients and families in need of our services. We started to admit clients at an unimaginable pace. We worked around the clock. God saw fit to bring on the staff members whom He knew would complement the level of care I desired for each client and their loved ones.

We were crazy busy! We became the preferred company in the building, even though there had been several others who had been providing the same kind of services before our arrival. We had thirteen clients, most of whom were in need of twenty-four-hour care. I was amazed at what was happening for all of us, because the staff members also deserved all that was happening on their behalf.

We were blessed beyond measure. For the second year while at the facility, WPS grossed around $400,000. Yes, from $48,000 to a significant surplus—an amount which left the accountant and payroll company stunned. I was exceptionally grateful to God for understanding every one of my shortcomings and recognizing that my desire to work in my field was always authentic. His generosity has continued on our behalf, as WPS has remained consistent with its earnings, and several of the staff members have stayed with me throughout the years. Also, our relationship with many of the staff members at the facility continues. Many of them have become our faithful supporters. My friendship with the man whom God destined to take me there flourished during the years, and we now call each other brother and sister. The admissions director became like a mother figure to me, and her inspiration, support, and belief in me are unparalleled.

In addition to these relationships, I became immensely blessed with the knowledge I gained from a couple of my clients who had been savvy business owners themselves in their early days. They took the time to share their wisdom to empower me to soar. We spent a considerable amount of time together one on one. I was extremely grateful for their dedication and support of me. While these two clients provided business knowledge, the rest provided some personal lessons that the staff members and I will use for the rest of our lives.

As I continued to marvel at my newfound success, I received a letter from the Georgia Department of Labor to inform me that my former employer from whom I had secured my unemployment benefit was challenging my claim. This issue had been something she had been fighting since it started, and now it was at its final stage. I had no choice but to respond to the order.

I contacted an attorney to assist me, because I did not know how to respond to a court order. It became a very long process, and in the end, I could not retain the attorney, as he was asking for a ridiculous amount of money. Having no other options, I challenged her claim on my own.

After a couple of hearings, I lost the case, and I was ordered to pay all of the unemployment benefits back. When the judgment was handed down, I laughed so hard, concluding that God had let me borrow the money in a time when I needed it the most, and that it was now time for me to repay it. I paid every penny I had received for unemployment back to the Georgia Department of Labor.

Yes, God does have a sense of humor.

In the end, I realize that God has given me endless possibilities for do-overs!

Chapter Five

Thou Art My God!

While in the process of writing this book, I contemplated whether to include an additional chapter about my Father and me. The reason is that my relationship with God deserves its own separate book entirely. Then, I realized that I have no guarantees that I may get to share it later in another book, so why not divulge some of our success stories now while I can?

You realized I said "success stories," correct? Yes, my relationship with my Father is one that I would without reservation categorize as my ultimate success story.

For over two decades I lived my life with the belief that my grandmother was the reason for the way my life had been. I credited almost all of my successes to her praying on my behalf, as well as the way she raised me. While her prayers are most definitely a contributing factor on how I was able to journey many of the roads I traveled, I have now come to know that God had been cooperating with her through His providence. His sanctifying grace has been the point of reference for my grandmother, which in turn flowed into me.

I did not understand the Bible verse of Jeremiah 1:5 until I went through some tumultuous times in my life, and yet His infinite grace continued to manifest itself, regardless of the situation. Jeremiah 1:5 became a reassuring verse for me that I could read and meditate on. It states, "Before I formed thee in the belly I knew thee; and before thou camest forth out of the womb I sanctified thee, and I ordained thee a prophet unto the nations" (KJV). Undoubtedly, the Lord was speaking to Jeremiah. I, too, have been called to be His servant, which makes me often wonder how He finds me worthy of His unmatched love, considering that I am a sinner.

I was in my early twenties when I had my first real encounter with God through a dream. I was at work one night when I dreamt I was wearing an orange jumpsuit and that I was in jail. In the dream, the voice speaking to me was telling me to pray. I woke up not knowing what to do, so I did nothing. Just as God was persistent at getting my attention, I was set on ignoring Him, because I did not listen, even though I had that very same dream every night for two weeks. I did not understand the relevance of the message to my life, because I knew I was not committing any crimes. Also, I did not owe anyone, nor was I stealing from anybody. *Why would I be in jail?* I asked myself.

Yes, I was aware that I was in an abusive relationship. Yet even then, I knew I was not in the wrong, as I was the one receiving the abuse. I was no match for my abuser, who was much taller and bigger than I was. With this mindset, I shrugged off the dream, because none of it made sense to me, anyway. I kept the dream to myself and continued on with life.

Then came the year 1998, when God's message became very clear to me.

I got into a fight with my then-boyfriend, Ian. This argument started because I asked for his share of our bills. I had been responsible for paying all of the bills, because his need for material things was more important than having a roof over our heads. It was now toward the end of the month; our bills were due, and I requested his part. Well, mentally he was already compromised by his recreational activity, and so came another assault, because I opened my mouth. This time, however, I needed to defend myself. If not, I was sure that I was going to die that day.

He overpowered me in the bedroom, and began to punch and kick me. I fought back and attempted to leave the apartment. He followed me into the living room. As we continued to struggle, we ended up in the kitchen, where he pinned me against the kitchen sink while grabbing me by the throat and suffocating me. I could feel my life fading away, so I reached over and grabbed a knife that was somewhere by the kitchen sink. I honestly can't remember how my hands were able to reach the knife. I stabbed him. I immediately ran out of the apartment and to his older sister's place about fifteen minutes away. Unbeknownst to me, I had stabbed him in his side and had punctured a lung. Thankfully, he was able to call his younger sister, who in turn called 911.

While I was at his older sister's place, I learned that they had admitted him, because his wound was severe. In that instant, I became a fugitive, because the police were now looking for me. A mutual friend of ours who knew a lot about our history decided to take me to another town an hour away. He was determined to save me from being victimized twice. I was motionless, still processing what had happened.

I stayed late into the night at his sister's place until I finally gave in to his advice of leaving town. Our friend was pleased I had accepted his suggestion, and we finally made the one-hour drive to his father's house.

Before long, the news spread like wildfire. Everyone was calling me to find out what had transpired. I did not respond. I needed to be still, so I ignored everyone. In my stillness, that small voice inside of me directed me to surrender myself. I listened and came out of the room where I had been resting to tell our friend that I was going to turn myself in to the police in the morning.

I woke up very early the next day and was ready to go. I was amazed at my sense of calm. We drove back to our town and went straight to the police station. When we arrived, our friend was not allowed to stay with me, because I was now under arrest. Two officers led me into an interrogation room, where they asked me to roleplay what had happened with one of them, which I did. I was truthful about what happened, so I had no concerns about demonstrating what occurred.

Well, my version was not good enough, apparently. They read me my Miranda rights and led me out of the room directly into a cell, where I spent the night. I don't remember if I slept at all, but I do know that I still had that sense of peace.

In the morning, an officer handcuffed me and advised me that he was taking me to the official jail in another town. I believe that the city was forty minutes away from where we lived. As the officer led me to his patrol car, he stopped to tighten the handcuffs on my wrists. Up until that moment, I had not done or said anything beyond adhering to their instructions. Right then, I knew all he cared about was getting a verdict for his city. I looked straight up at him and said, "Sir, please understand that I am not a criminal. I came to you voluntarily, and so I have no desire to run."

I will never forget the look on his face. He looked at me, but didn't say a word. He then loosened the tight grip he had on my wrists and assisted me into the back of his vehicle.

As we drove, I focused my gaze at the trees and admired all of nature's beauty. Although I was unaffected by all that was happening to me at that time, I became embarrassed when we stopped at a traffic light, and I made eye contact with a young lady about my age. I felt ashamed. At that moment, the realization of my position became apparent.

When we finally arrived at the jail, he handed me over to that jurisdiction and left. I was now in another town, alone, and being booked into another jail for who knows how long. After going through all the motions, I was given an orange jumpsuit and asked to change. Yes, the event I had been dreaming about for weeks prior was now a reality.

I spent a few days on one side of the jail before I was released because I had no prior record. I was let out on my own accord and given a court date to appear. Ian's younger sister came to pick me up. By then, I had lost about half my weight, because I could not eat the food.

Following my release, I had a list of restrictions that I could not violate or else I would be thrown back in jail immediately. Two conditions were that I could not return home due to a no-contact order between Ian and me, and that I had to surrender my passport.

Well, Ian and I lived together in the home that I had been the primary provider for. Afraid of violating the court order, I was forced to make other living arrangements, so I stayed with his younger sister until I was able to find myself another apartment. Also, I needed to find an attorney, which I was able to do.

I continued to work at the same place, so I devoted myself to work. It was also during this time that Ian's family began to share details with me of what they had known about the incident. Another older sister of his had taken him to the police station, and they both had provided false statements of what had occurred. It was their version against mine.

This particular sister did not get along well with me. She had voiced on several occasions that she wished that I would die. She did a whole lot more than I care to dignify in my writing. The rest of his family, though, supported me wholeheartedly, for which I was immensely grateful.

They did not let the bond that they shared as a family undermine the truth. They were aware of our history and knew how much I had endured from Ian. Before this particular incident, he had put his hands on me on several occasions. He had already had encounters with the law, though, and if I had reported him, it would have compromised his education and overall life.

Nevertheless, Ian did not extend this same courtesy to me, as he willingly sided with his sister to lie about what occurred. I then concluded that in the dream, God had been trying to tell me that it was time to leave, but I had failed to listen, mostly because of my ignorance in His regard.

It is ironic to share that even in the middle of everything, I did not think of praying and seeking His guidance. Instead, I relied on my Mamma's prayers, as she had always prayed on my behalf, and the support of his family to get me through.

My attorney was now working with the prosecutor's office to reach a plea bargain. These negotiations went on forever, it seemed. For some reason, I did not share what was happening to me with my family back in Sierra Leone, until one afternoon. I was home alone in my new apartment when that still small voice whispered that I should call my grandmother to share how my life had changed. I did.

I called Mamma and told her everything. I shared some of the many ways Ian's mother and the rest of his family had supported me during this ordeal. Mamma ordered me to shield myself from all of it and to begin praying. She told me that the only one who could save me was God. At that moment, His name became a prominent stamp in my life. I did as Mamma had ordered me. After all, I trusted her with my life, so I had no reservation with honoring her directive.

As my attorney continued to work on my behalf, I began to pray the best way I knew how, which in essence was a baby's prayer: reciting what little praying words I had learned as a child. Nevertheless, it became apparent that He did not care whether I was a proficient prayer or not. He just wanted my attention, so He could teach me how to build a relationship with Him. Marveled by all of it, I prayed faithfully, and He, in turn, was faithful at guiding my attorney.

My attorney was worried that deportation was imminent, because accusations such as those that I was facing were subject to deportation if I was found guilty at trial. My attorney and I met on many occasions while he was going back and forth with the prosecutor in negotiation. I knew that Mamma was always praying on my behalf, so I remained calm.

My attorney called me one afternoon and said the prosecutor had drastically reduced the charges from felonies to misdemeanors. There were three charges, to be exact. He continued to tell me that the prosecutor was not going to seek deportation. I could hear the excitement in his voice. Honestly, I didn't know the difference between having a felony record and a misdemeanor record except that one was better than the other.

He advised, "Ms. Jaka, you should take this deal." I inquired as to why I should plead guilty when I was defending myself. He responded, "Ms. Jaka, the prosecuting office believes the story that your boyfriend and his sister told the officers. It's your word against theirs." Finally, he said, "Take the deal, and you won't go to trial."

I agreed.

The day came when I was supposed to go to court to enter a plea. My attorney had advised that I plead nolo contendere, which is similar to a no-contest plea. He rallied support from some of my friends and some of Ian's family members to write letters on my behalf.

On the day of my hearing, Ian's mother, who at the time had been diagnosed with cancer and was frail while undergoing treatment, came to court with me to enter my plea. As fragile and compromised as she was, she was determined to support me. God was on my side! When it was my turn, I entered my plea. My attorney was very nervous, as a plea bargain did not finalize the case. For some reason, he acted like he had been commissioned to save me, an attitude I now credit to God's divine intervention.

The judge had the outcome of what would become of me. Well, I knew who *really* was in charge. By now, my Mamma had shared with me who had the final say. I was composed.

After all the formality, the judge entered her final order. I was ordered to spend thirty days in jail with work release and placed on three years' probation. Interestingly, it still felt like I was dreaming, because I was yet again very calm. In the judge's order, she provided me some time before I had to turn myself in. In the end, we left and went home.

On the drive home, Ian's mother apologized profusely. I could feel her hurt for me. Her level of sincerity pierced my heart. I was grateful. Upon our return, we shared what had happened, so the rest of his family and our friends wanted to immediately shield me from what they thought would potentially break me. I was appreciative of their thoughtfulness. Nevertheless, I was now focused on myself and what had become of me. Most importantly, I had other matters to attend to, so I went home alone.

I continued to work. I also continued to pray as best as I knew how. I did not share with my family back home the outcome of my case, because I did not want them to worry about me. I kept my routine as usual until it was time for me to surrender myself.

When the time came for me to report to jail, Ian's sister drove me to the facility where I had been ordered to serve my sentence. We hugged and said our goodbyes. I don't remember how I felt, but upon exiting the car, I proudly walked in and went through the processing, and eventually I was booked. I began serving my thirty days. I was in a section that, instead of cells, simply had a very large space with bunk beds all around. I was always worried that I'd fall out of my bed, as I had the top bunk. It was a hard iron bed with no support, and I needed to be very careful. We had two shower stalls that provided very little privacy. I was grateful, however, that I could leave for a total of eight hours, to include driving time per day, for five days a week for work.

Yes, God was gracious to me, indeed.

My prison journey was going well, until my relief from work was late one evening. My coworker caused me to be a few minutes past the time of my scheduled return. Upon my arrival, the intake officer was beyond nasty toward me. I tried to explain that my coworker had arrived late and that I could not leave the individuals we worked with unattended. She took my response to mean that I was challenging her authority, and threatened to send me to the other side where I had been before my hearing, and to revoke my work privilege. In that instant, I became a submissive child. I apologized and humbled myself, because she was one who needed her ego stroked. My approach worked.

During my thirty days in jail, I did not make any friends, nor did I eat the food. I did not have an appetite, which made a couple of the ladies happy, since they got to eat my meals. Also, I did not know the environment, so I was unsure on how to navigate my surroundings. I spent most of my time on my bed being still. Again, I was still at the beginning stages of my relationship with God, and so I did not even devote my spare time in prayer with Him as I should have, but I prayed.

In the end, I completed my full thirty days and was released.

Now an ex-convict, I didn't know how it'd affect the rest of my life. What I did know was that I was thankful that I had an opportunity for a fresh start. I was able to complete all of the requirements, which included my monthly supervisory visit to my probation officer for three long years, and I paid all of the restitution to the court that I was ordered to pay.

Moreover, I had a hefty amount that I owed my attorney. Nonetheless, he was very kind to me. He understood my position, so he allowed me to pay him half of what my entire total would have been.

As I continued in my routine, I realized that God had interrupted my story, and so I was eager to find out what was next on His agenda for me.

Chapter Six

"Your Word, O Lord, Is Truth; Consecrate Us in the Truth"

A change was undoubtedly happening for me. Nevertheless, as I continued with my life, I was still struggling with the specifics of how my life should change, because after all, I had no clear map for what my new beginning should be. My shift had come while I was in an abusive relationship with Ian. Up until then, I thought I had everything under control. I was independent, and I knew that I was very responsible.

Nonetheless, there was one area of my life that kept repeating itself: my attraction to men who devalued my worth by the way they treated me. This dysfunctional part of my life was all I had come to know. Before my relationship with Ian, another ex-boyfriend had abused me, which was something I never shared with anyone. Although it was never anything close to what I endured with Ian, I still suffered abuse in that relationship. It was clear that I didn't know any different.

Furthermore, I did not have a role model to teach me what was acceptable or unacceptable when I became an adult involved in intimate relationships. The lack of formal guidance and a clear vision prevented me from quickly grasping what to do and how to be better. Unsure of what else could be so different, I positioned myself to learn what was contrary to what I had accepted for myself.

I was eager to hear from God again. I continued to pray as usual. I didn't do anything drastic regarding my prayer habit, but at least I had come to know His name and would occasionally revere Him. Nothing happened between He and me. I forgot all about our first encounter and continued living my life. Years passed before I would hear from Him again, which is not to say He had not been silently present every step of the way.

I was twenty-eight years old when He graced me with His presence again. I had just given birth to my daughter. As I juggled the tasks of motherhood, He decided that it'd be the perfect time to visit with me. It was late in the evening when I became sick very suddenly. Throughout the day, I was doing fine and had gone about my normal routine. However, toward the evening hours, I started trembling, and a heavy fever came upon me. It was only my daughter and me at home. I managed to do what I had to do on her behalf, and we settled into bed. As we lay there, she began to cry, because she wanted to be in my arms. I picked her up and held her on my chest. I was not yet asleep, as I was trying to nurse myself from what was an unusual illness, so I remember this incident with all clarity.

I was still overwhelmed by how I was feeling and could not understand what was happening to me. Immediately after that, I began to shake uncontrollably. In that instance, Jesus, dressed in a white robe, appeared in front of me and extended His hand, as if He wanted me to take hold of it. I started to sweat profusely as I continued to tremble, so much so that I thought I was going to drop my infant daughter to the floor. He continued to stretch His hand toward me, but I refused to extend mine. This episode went on for what seemed like minutes. Regrettably, He disappeared as I continued to decline to extend my hand to His.

I did not know what to make of the encounter. Astonished, I lay there motionless in dismay until I finally fell asleep. The next morning when I woke up, everything was normal, as if nothing had transpired the night before. I was well again.

I do not know why Jesus appeared to me. Also, I did not have the spiritual ability to ask. I was still in an infancy stage of my relationship with Him, and thus lacked the understanding of the profound depth of Him gracing me with His presence.

A few days after Jesus appeared to me, my brother Richmond passed away. Then I became curious about His visit. I asked Him in a one-on-one conversation if He had come to take me home that day, and because I had refused, He took Richmond instead. It is a question that I have asked Him from time to time throughout the years, and it is one that He's yet to answer.

Coincidentally, not long after Jesus appeared to me, I had another encounter with someone from the Holy Family. I was on the couch in my living room one afternoon just relaxing. It was a bright and sunny day outside. As I lay there peacefully, I realized that there was a shadow on the wall by the front door. I turned and looked over, and saw the face of the Blessed Virgin Mary on the wall right where the shadow was. This image rested there for a little while, as if I needed to get a clear picture of it. There were no exchanges, but instead, her visit was a quiet one, and eventually she disappeared.

I had not shared with anyone that Jesus had appeared to me, but when the Blessed Virgin Mary did, I felt I needed to tell someone. I beckoned Ian's mother from the other room and shared that I had seen the Blessed Virgin Mary. Her response was something I will never forget. She turned to me and said, "You are not an ordinary child."

I was baffled at her remark. What did she mean by that? Sure, I was ignorant concerning God, but I felt that her statement demonstrated an understanding that she could not have possibly known on her own. She had been around me for several years before Jesus and the Blessed Virgin Mary appeared to me, so how could she now conclude that I was not an ordinary child? I became mystified by it all. Her response sounded as if she were being instructed to pass on a message to me. My antenna went up; I was all ears, ready to listen.

I formed a conclusion that day that there had to be a profound reason why Jesus and the Blessed Mother had appeared to me. I was eager to know what would come next regarding my relationship with the Ever-Living God. I knew something divine was at play because of these events and the statement made by Ian's mother, all of which preset events of what would continue to happen between my Heavenly Father and me. God was shifting me!

Before I got married, my relationship with Him was one that I would refer to as a very casual relationship. Although He was always present and leading my every step, I was busy thanking my Mamma, and I had only come to know Him through her directive when I was in trouble. In turn, He set the stage for me to know that while my grandmother had been on the forefront, He was the divine master who is the author of my life. The shift in my life was evident by the relationships He established for the rest of my journey.

My then-husband was very prayerful. He was ten steps ahead of me in his relationship with God. He prayed and often fasted, which was a routine I became a part of, as well. We had many challenges in our marriage, but our time with God was uncompromised. Through his discipline, I was able to begin building a closer relationship with God. In turn, I learned how to pray more than I knew how before.

During this time, I started working as a certified nursing assistant with an elderly lady who needed support. My relationship with my client was going well for the first few years. However, it became apparent that things were changing between us. I had worked for this client for over two and a half years. In my third year of working with her, my then-husband and I were also working on me gaining my permanent residency in the United States. Thus, we were fasting, and our prayer life had increased. It was imperative that we devote ourselves to this level of intimacy with God, because the attorney whom we had hired had suggested that I do nothing regarding my change of status. My conviction had put me in jeopardy for deportation. Even though the prosecutor had not sought deportation when I was convicted, per the immigration attorney, submitting any requests on my behalf for an adjustment of status would be cause for deportation.

As I stated, my then-husband was a prayerful man, and he had confidence in God's ability. I had caught the praying bug myself. It was during this time that I began to take my Bible to work, as I needed to read the daily scriptures we had chosen during our fast. It was a decision that almost caused me to lose my mind. Chaos engulfed my entire being. I had no idea what was happening to me as I was thrust suddenly into two different worlds at the same time.

While I was at work, I would read the Bible upon my arrival for at least thirty minutes, because my client required that I allow her time to wake up on her own. I took advantage of the spare time . . . so I thought. As I began to read the Bible and pray one morning, something strange happened. Suddenly, I became stiff and was unable to move or speak. My entire body was numb, which lasted for a few minutes. I did not know what to make of this, so I continued with my day as usual.

When I got home, I shared with my then-husband what had happened. He shared that he believed that the attack was a nightmare.

Nightmare? What?

It was a new terminology for me, as I had not experienced it before. Moreover, it was in the daytime. In my opinion, nightmares imply nighttime. He went on to explain that it had to do with an evil force. Okay! Now, I was curious.

Evil force? Wait, what? Why me, and why at work?

We talked it all out, and he gave me a better understanding of its meaning, and we settled the matter. I was not at all concerned with this opposition, so I continued my routine of reading the Bible in the morning when I arrived at work. Well, the same episode continued every time. The more I was attacked, the harder I prayed and the more vigorously I read the Bible. At the same time, I began to dream of my client most days, which made our encounters at her house even stranger. I was in a brutal conflict with something unfamiliar.

One day, I had a dream in which God showed my client as the attacker. In it, she was challenging me by saying that I would never be able to leave her and that I belonged to her "kingdom." She further offered me all of her riches if I would accept to be part of her "world." I challenged her in return, and I said that I did not belong to her. Needless to say, she and I were on the opposite sides of the kingdoms. By now, I knew that I belonged to the Almighty God and she to . . . whomever.

She and I continued this fight for about six months. I was mentally and physically exhausted. It seemed that God wanted me to endure, as the battle was His. In return, he was strengthening me spiritually.

Finally, one day I abruptly called my supervisor to share that I was resigning. I explained what had transpired between my client and me. To my surprise, my supervisor explained that she, too, had worked for a client with whom she had experienced the same, and so she did not doubt my experience.

Yes, you guessed it. My former client was persistent. She called me and my employer repeatedly to state that she needed me back, and she refused to accept another caregiver. But, I never returned to work for her.

These events were not all that God allowed as He drew me closer to Him. As my then-husband and I continued in our quest for me to obtain my green card, we faced many discouraging outcomes. The attorney had advised that I stay on the "downlow" and lead a low-key life. Regardless of the attorney's opinion on the matter, I had come to know that God had a different plan for me.

We continued to pray and fast, and I began to dream about specific events in my life and what God wanted me to do in this regard. Many of the dreams I remember to this day. A couple of them are of much significance to me, as they clearly detail how much God loves me. One in particular was of someone speaking to me, telling me how much God loves me, but I had "done some things to disappoint Him." Nevertheless, at the same time, the same voice continued to tell me that I should continue to pray and that the Lord was ready to bless me. Furthermore, the voice shared that God's love for me was like someone in the Bible. Sadly, when I woke up, I could not remember the name of the person who the voice referenced in the Bible.

I was amazed at what had happened. When I woke up, I shared the dream with my then-husband. I began to pray more, and I often fasted, too. All the while, it felt as if I were in dreamland, as messages in my dreams were becoming more evident in the direction of where I needed to focus myself. By now, I knew that God had spoken, so I should not let my limitations or fear paralyze me. I told my then-husband that we should return to the attorney and ask to file my papers, regardless of what was advised. He listened.

We set up an appointment with the attorney. During our meeting, the attorney and paralegal were a bit taken aback by my confident demeanor. Because I had come to know myself and whom the world belonged to, I was fearless. The attorney complied, and we began the process.

God was in control! He continued to direct me by illustrating a clear picture of events through my dreams of how I should proceed with the immigration process and the attorney. The most miraculous of all was when He shared what I should wear for my interview with US Citizenship and Immigration Services, and what He was going to do on the day of my interview. In this particular dream, I was instructed to wear light-gray pants and a light-blue shirt with a white collar. Furthermore, it was revealed that it was going to rain and thunder during my interview, which would be a sign to me.

When I woke up, needless to say, I was determined to find light-gray pants and a light-blue shirt with a white collar. I raced to the mall, going from store to store. Thankfully, I was able to find my outfit. I purchased what I had been instructed to wear and paired it with black high heels. (Back then, I was a few pounds lighter than I am now, so I still have the shirt in my closet, but I gave the pants away because my hips got wider.)

In the meantime, everything with my paperwork was going well. Every submission got an approval, up until the day for my interview. The big day came along, and we were ready. I had purchased Marvin Sapp's CD entitled "Thirsty." His song "Never Would've Made It" had become my anthem. I hid the CD in the glove compartment, as I intended to play that song after the interview. We got ready, I wore my outfit, and we prayed before heading out the door.

We arrived very early that day and waited for a long time. Finally, our time came.

A young immigration officer came out and called us. We followed him into his office. I was calm. That sense of calm that had been with me in those times of trouble was yet again present at that moment. I was not nervous at all.

As we made ourselves comfortable, the officer started the interview by cracking jokes. Indeed, God was in control, because it did not feel as if we were at a meeting with the Department of Immigration. As the formal interview began, it began to thunder and rain. I looked outside and smiled. I also pinched my then-husband's leg to remind him of the dream that I had shared with him. At that point, I knew God had bestowed His grace upon me!

Our interview was brief. The officer brought up my criminal conviction. As he began the conversation, his focus quickly shifted to how different my accent was compared to other people from Sierra Leone. I shared that being raised in Italy played a role in how I speak. We then started talking about our different upbringings and family life. As we concluded the interview, the rain and thunder stopped. Suddenly, I recognized that God had done what He had said He was going to do. At that moment, His love captured me! My heart was full of gratitude. As I continued to be mesmerized at His all-surpassing ability, the officer shared that he was going to approve my application, which would grant me my green card.

Now, from what I knew based on conversations with the attorney and others, a final decision was left with the Department of

Immigration to approve all applicants' petitions, which could be on the day of the interview or via mail at a later date. Miraculously, I gained my approval on the very same day.

It became God's word versus that of my attorney. She had advised that I do nothing, while God said, "Go ahead. I've got you." By faith and confidence in His mighty name, I chose to believe God's directive, and in the end, His word reigned supreme. This belief He instructed His son Solomon to write all those years ago in Proverbs 3:26 (KJV), so we, too, can become believers of it: "For the Lord shall be thy confidence, and shall keep thy foot from being taken."

We left feeling overjoyed. As we got in the car, I pulled out the CD and inserted it in the CD player. My then-husband, surprised, asked, "You bought his CD?" I smiled as I blasted the song "Never Would've Made It," which I had on repeat throughout the drive home. It didn't just stop there. I played it so much that Camilla, who was an infant at the time, knew every word to the song and could sing it verbatim.

Chapter Seven

Forever Desperate for My Heavenly Father's Touch

The events I have shared are just a few of those that have transpired between my Father and me. He has continued to afford me opportunities to learn about my life, as well as others'. My abilities to dream and see visions are gifts that I do not take lightly. Although I have met with opposition and denial from time to time by friends, family, the men I have dated, and even acquaintances who would outright question the validity of His messages to me, I have never been deterred from sharing His word. After all, I, too, did not adhere to it when He first spoke to me in a dream.

My dreams are often too direct and somewhat frightening. Moreover, the visions or dreams don't require that I have a special relationship with someone in order for me to dream of events that are going to happen or that are happening around that person, which usually don't pertain to me. It just has to be that he or she associates with me, so I do understand their position of rejection, which is justified.

I mean, at the beginning stages of my relationship with Him, I would have been doubtful myself, especially if someone with whom I had little or no affiliation would have shared events about my life that are presumably going to happen or that are happening. Good grief! Rejection would not have been my only opposition, but I would have concluded that he or she might have been abnormal. Nevertheless, God knows how to grab the attention of those whom He has set aside for His purpose.

It is very fitting that I share these events here, as they have helped some of my family members believe on some level. My younger cousin had accepted that she was not going to be able to conceive a child, as doctors had reported to her. One day I dreamt that my cousin was going to have a child. I shared the dream with her and she, in turn, shared the dream with her family. As time went on, she became pregnant and gave birth to a beautiful baby girl, who is now ten years of age.

The same goes for some friends and acquaintances who have had the same or even greater experiences of what God can do. Most recently, I had a dream about my cousin in California. When I woke up, I sent him a text about what I dreamt. He texted me back right away and said his girlfriend was pregnant and was amazed that I had dreamt about it, because they had not shared this information with anyone. He, too, was one who'd been skeptical about God's messages, based on the many arguments we have had over the years. Nevertheless, his position has changed on some level, but I believe that God shared his private information with me so he could shift his perspective about His divine abilities.

Similar events have changed how many of my family and friends receive God's messages—most importantly, who God can use to deliver a message that is worthy of their hearing. Of course, not everyone has fully embraced my God-given gifts, and so I often share my own experiences to get them to at least consider. When this happens, I am grateful. On those occasions when I am not successful at God's message resonating with others, I move on, as God clearly says in John 10:27 (KJV), "My sheep hear my voice, and I know them, and they follow me." Therefore, the result becomes between them and God.

As for me, I am most grateful that He has allowed me to master the audacity of hope and allow my faith in Him to mature. By Him grooming and having the level of patience He has had with me, I have now come to believe in the Bible verse Romans 4:21 (EST) that says, "Fully convinced that God was able to do what He had promised."

My life has been a roller-coaster ride. I have had my ups and my downs, and I have journeyed through places and endured trials and tribulations, all of which have afforded me the liberation to surrender in being His precious daughter. His pruning of me has increased my prayer life tremendously. However, I won't dare boast that I have become proficient at praying. Nevertheless, I have mastered the kind of prayer that I believe God is most appreciative of. While I have learned to devote time in prayer and worship, and have made it a priority to attend church regularly, I have come to believe that I am most useful in my praise when I utter these three simple words throughout the day: "Thank you, Father!" When I think of the roads we have traveled, and all that He has done for me, these three little words serve as a constant reminder of what He deserves from me, and so I am never too tired of saying it.

Thank you, Father!

Through God's infinite grace, I am no longer in bondage to my past experiences. His grace has been made sufficient in me (2 Corinthians 12:9, NIV). His intercessor, the Holy Spirit, affords me the ability to be still when the world around me is in chaos. I have centered myself on His promises when life's challenges become too hard for me to bear. Our history has positioned me to journey every single day in His confidence. He promised that He would never leave, nor will He ever forsake me (Hebrews 13:5), and thus, I will forever be desperate for His touch.

In closing, this Bible verse that I have chosen to share eloquently summarizes my relationship with my Heavenly Father: "All things are done according to God's plan and decision; and God chose us to be his own people in union with Christ because of his own purpose, based on what he had decided from the very beginning" (Ephesians 1:11, GNT).

Chapter Eight

Dearest Camilla

Dearest Camilla,

To say I love you beyond words would be an understatement . . .

I didn't know that I would be scrambling to gather my thoughts as I began writing this chapter of ours. I never knew it'd be this difficult to share what it means to have you in my life. Perhaps it is because you are such an amazing daughter that I would want to honor our experiences by sharing our journey in the most humble way possible.

You are an extraordinary child! I could not be more proud of the assignment that God called me on to be your mother. He knew that we would match perfectly.

I remember when I first became pregnant with you. It was a surprise, but I instantly knew that I was going to bring you into this world against all odds. I was unprepared, but something about your arrival gave me the audacity to be different. It didn't matter that I had no clear vision of what my life would be like with you in it. None of that mattered. Something about you brought clarity into my life, and so I was determined to move Heaven and earth to make sure our story was one of success.

You changed me!

Everything about you is perfect. I've asked God on several occasions how He saw me fit to be an instrument in your life. Before you came, I was going through the motions and riding the waves of this thing called life. I was clueless about the expectations of becoming a woman, but then God gracefully saw fit to pair you with me, because He knew that you would secretly be my point of reference.

Your arrival taught me that I had a voice. I had been navigating through life with the broken pieces of what had become of me, because I was submissive to the opinions of others, particularly the young men I dated. I devalued my womanhood, and I permitted them to dictate my worth and treat me with very little respect and honor. I was a lost soul desperate to belong. I lacked almost everything these relationships provided me. My desire to have a family unit, amazing friends, and the types of relationships I wanted while growing up all caused me to accept the value they placed on my womanhood. In my incompleteness, I could not refute what they believed of me, because I knew no different.

You changed all of that, and I have not been the same ever since. Your little life came to reposition my adult life in what would be the best thing that could have happened to me. Since your arrival, you have challenged me to be the best version of myself. I don't believe you know how inspired I am because of who you are. Everything about you sets you apart from what I've known. I am not sure that you are aware of how often I would look at you and not say a word. It is because I am so grateful that God blessed me with one of His little angels who has such a profound effect on my life. You are the halo of light that God sent to come brighten my life.

From an infant to now, having evolved into a spectacular young lady, you haven't changed much. Instead, you have continued to build on your foundation. You have always been a sweet child who is caring, respectful, and loving. I admire your sense of humor, which is something that many people don't know about you. I often share with others that there are two Camillas: the one who is soft-spoken, polite, and caring in public or while at other people's homes, and the one who yanks my chain at home with her impressive sense of self.

You are hilarious! Your funny jokes and quick comebacks are priceless. Your sense of humor is one to die for. You are, by all accounts, an undiscovered comedian. I treasure the funny moments of our lives that you have allowed me to cultivate—most importantly, the ones where you so eloquently tell me while I try to offer advice, "Woman, it's not about you." Or, when you are irritated with something I have done or said, I'll get it again: "Woman, what's with you?"

You are a character. I treasure all that God has allowed us to cultivate as mother and daughter. We have been blessed to have a different outcome than that of my mother and me, and I wouldn't change anything about our history thus far.

As a child, I lacked what you and I have. My childhood differs significantly from yours, so my goal is to be the best mother I can be and to set the best example for you. I understand that most times you are unable to grasp the lessons I try to pass on to you, because you often think that I have lost my mind. I get it fully. Many times, I do forget that you are all but fourteen years of age. Nevertheless, I admire your tenacity.

You are wise far beyond your years, and your analytical mind usually leaves me in dismay. You always fascinate me with your responses while I attempt to provide you with watered-down answers to many of your questions that often make you say, "Really, Mommy?" In those instances, I aim to shield you from those areas of my life that I am not proud of, and most importantly, I do not want to give you the excuse to repeat my mistakes.

While I was growing up, I needed my mother. She was unavailable, because she, too, was a child. I was blessed, however, to have had my Mamma, who gave everything she had in raising my siblings and me. My relationship with her is one that I have shared with you and that you have come to know very well.

I know that you are still confused as to why my relationship with my mother is far different from ours. Furthermore, your question as to why I do not call my mother "Mommy" is something I have never been able to adequately answer. It saddens me that I can only answer your questions based on my understanding of what transpired between my mother and me. I am well aware that my answers still leave you confused, because your face and body language often reflect how you feel.

Camilla, I believe that not having my mother around as a child has served as a blessing. My void continues to be the motivating factor for me to be all that God has called me to be on your behalf. That emptiness that I have carried with me throughout the years serves as my inspiration to mother you with everything I have. You see, my lack has provided an opportunity to develop something unique for us.

While I try to raise you to have values, morals, dignity, and honor, as well as to develop good characteristics that will enable you to soar, it is also my responsibility to protect your innocence. I know that you often believe that I am different from other mothers whom you are blessed to have in your life and for whom I am entirely grateful. My experiences differ significantly from theirs. Nonetheless, you are still a child, and so I do not expect you to understand fully. Because of that, I often swallow my feelings of disappointment when you refer to me as a "mean mother." It hurts me secretly, but I know how much I desire for you.

The pain I have carried around all these years keeps me

focused on ensuring that your experiences differ from mine. I have taken a lot of left turns, many due to bad decisions, but other events were created for me by adults whom both Mamma and my mother trusted. In turn, I am as "mean as a nail," as you often tell me, because I am responsible for your overall well-being. I would never want you to experience many of the things I have experienced. For this, I make no apologies.

My goal is to shield you from many of the things I have endured, and so I can never afford myself the opportunity to be different from how I am raising you now. I will forever be a "mean mother" if this keeps you from making the mistakes I made or be a victim of the things I fell victim to. If it keeps you from accepting anything less than what you deserve, and if it empowers you to define yourself by the values that God is allowing you to cultivate, then I am a "mean mother" for life.

I desire for you to have a voice that is unique to your identity. I aim for you to never conform to pleasing others that aren't worthy of you. I am a "mean mother" because you are a precious gem, and thus I will continue to be the voice that reminds you that God has marked you with a purpose.

Unlike you, I did not come to know my value until I had been abused and used for the benefit of others. I almost lost my life and freedom before God allowed me to discover my sense of self. Therefore, I am tremendously grateful that God turned my life around in preparation for your arrival and has been using me as a channel to help direct your steps.

Before now, there are areas of my life that I haven't shared with you out of fear of overloading you with too much at such a young age. Also, I was fearful and ashamed, because I didn't know to whom I could share my truth without being judged. I was certain that if I told my mom or grandmother, they wouldn't have known how to receive me or my story as a child. But truthfully, I did not share because I had often wondered if both my Mamma and mother were also victims like me, mainly because child abuse is somewhat prominent in my country, and almost no one ever talks about it.

Because of you, I now need to change my course and expose myself to the only person who deserves to know part of the reason I have earned the title "mean mom." Perhaps you can now understand the zeal I possess to keep you protected. Maybe my truth will now help you understand some of my "mean" ways as I continue to do my best in raising you to become a woman of substance.

I remember like it was yesterday when I began to teach you about your private parts and what was appropriate and what wasn't. You were barely three years of age when I started to educate and empower you to speak up and to never be afraid to share anything with me. I feel blessed that those teachings have now transcended into a level of open communication between you and me. I value what we have developed, especially how secure you feel in talking to me openly.

I was not yet five years old when two adult males molested me. We lived in the home where I was born with several others in the compound. I confirmed with my mother the year we moved from this location. She shared that it was in 1982. I was born in 1976. I remember these events vividly. These men were tailors who sewed clothes for a living, and they rented the shop in front of the complex and lived in the back of one of the units. They took a particular interest in me and would always have me in their home. I remember as a child, both of them taking turns molesting and raping me time and time again.

I remember one particular day while one of them was molesting me, my older brother Richmond screamed my name as my family looked for me. I remember this man rushing to get me cleaned up before my brother got to his place. He hastily pushed me out the door, and I just collided with my brother at the man's front door. Thankfully, I was not hurt from the man forcefully pushing me out in his attempt for my brother to not discover what he was doing to me. My brother took me by the hand, and we walked back to our place as if nothing had happened.

Many more of these incidents happened, and over time, these episodes have played in my head over and over again. The memories have never faded away. As a child, I was unaware that the actions of those men were wrong, and that both of them had violated me by taking away my innocence.

I have often asked myself how my Mamma and mother didn't know what was happening to me. After all, they were responsible for me, so how they could have missed the signs is something that has baffled me over the years. A part of me is resentful toward them for failing to protect me. These incidents have caused me a significant level of pain that I have attempted to mend on my own, but still stirs up from time to time. I have forgiven both my Mamma and mother for failing me in this regard, but the pain is still evident.

Sweetheart, many of my behaviors stem from my experiences.

Having been molested as a child is one area of my life that has left me feeling paranoid on your behalf, and so I go the extra mile to shelter you from experiencing the same. Furthermore, I have been the subject of abuse. As much as I would like to hide this from you, it wouldn't be right, as I am unveiling every part of the woman that is your mother.

In my past relationships, I was the subject of both physical and emotional abuse by men who claimed to love me. I *haven't always been this wise. I know you believe that I am smart, as you so often tell me. What you don't know is that my intelligence developed after many poor decisions and mistakes.*

I learned how to navigate many of the roads I traveled by failing time and time again. I thought I had self-confidence, but truly that was a coping mechanism that I had developed on my own. Unlike you, I earned my intelligence through many tears. Thus, I am overbearing in order to keep you from experiencing many of my painful mistakes. I thank God that even with the little attitude that you give me, you are receptive of what I am passing on to you. I know this because your body language gives you away, which, by the way, helps me to see that I am getting through to you.

I pray that by me emptying myself to you, you receive my truth and use it to seek something different. I desire for you to never choose a boyfriend or husband who would think less of you—or himself, for that matter—or perpetuate any types of abuse toward you. Abuse comes in many forms, so please be alert. I didn't know any better. I had no role model to teach me differently. But, I thank God that you do. You have no excuse to not use your power to refute what is contrary to what you have learned. God has given you the spirit of discernment, so I want you to reject what the enemy would try to feed you with enthusiasm. Never settle for less than what you are worth. Be fierce and independent, but also know how to work cooperatively with everyone. Be humble in all you do, because humility is virtue.

In your little life, you have had two crushes: one in elementary school and another in middle school. For both, there were competitions, as you and your friends liked the same boys. Unfortunately, it doesn't get easier, as this does happen sometimes in adulthood, as well. However, always know your value. Never diminish your worth, and never settle to please other people. When you begin to date, if the person you are dating is unable or unwilling to be involved in a monogamous relationship with you, then he's not worthy of you and he's not the right one. You are enough; assume your position with grace and honor! Never undervalue who you are in order to fit into someone else's make-believe box of how you should be. You have virtues; hold fast to them.

As young as you are, you have seen me fall on several occasions, but you have also seen the power of God's love and mercy in our lives. You have watched me mend heartbreaks, even though I try to shield you from them, but you are too wise and nothing gets past you. In my moments of tribulations, you understood enough—so much that in your little subtle ways, you provided me comfort and understanding. You are always able to tell when I am not at my best, and you'll ask, "Are you mad about something? Because you are cranky." Nothing hides from your little eyes!

I'll forever treasure our experiences, for they have shaped both you and me into one fantastic duo. My life would be incomplete without you in it. Your level of intelligence and wisdom far exceeds all of your fourteen years on this earth. As I watch you grow, I am amazed at your ability to grasp the expectations of life with the level of confidence that you demonstrate. Granted, I have been your mother, and we both have been blessed to have each other. Nonetheless, your level of independence is something to be admired.

I take no credit for the things that God is doing in your life. You are His, and I am His instrument. I am immensely grateful that the two of you have your own relationship and that you have come to know who is your "ride or die" as you continue to journey your course. Never cease to trust in God or in His ability. He is the GPS that you are always going to need as you continue to live your life.

I am thankful for the gifts that He has bestowed upon you, even beyond your academic achievements. You are compassionate and thoughtful. Your level of empathy and love for others often leaves me in awe. I am proud of the young lady that you are. Never change who you are, but in the event that you do, let it be that you desire to be more than you already are.

My continued prayer for you is that you will forever channel the zest of faith and perseverance God has given you, and that you never conform to the voices that say that you are not good enough. Remember God's word that says you are more than a conqueror (Romans 8:37). I will continue to pray that you dream beyond the horizon, and that God's grace forever befalls you and guides your every footstep. May nothing more and nothing less than what God has purposed for your life be manifested in you.

Above all else, I pray that you will guard your heart, for everything you do will flow from it (Proverbs 4:23, NIV).

Love endlessly,
Your Forever Woman

Chapter Nine

Dear Future Husband

Dear future husband,

In anticipation of your arrival, I desire to share my truths in hopes that it will help you to love me as I deserve to be loved. Life's journeys have prepared me to be the most precious gift you will ever receive. Please strive to understand these virtues of mine, as I desire not to have to settle nor compromise any of them. I, too, will adhere to and honor all of your virtues throughout eternity.

I am sure you might contemplate not reading this, as it may frighten you. But you see, to date, I have attempted on several occasions these things called love and relationships. I continue to get the same results, even though I have managed to ask all the right questions and express my expectations and desires very clearly. If you decide to read this letter before your proposal, I am sure then that you, too, must have endured some of the same failures as it pertains to love and relationships.

Please allow me to introduce myself. I believe in God, and my relationship with Him is a priority. I am sensitive, fragile, and at times very timid, to the point that I could be considered antisocial. I have minimal social skills and often fail to cultivate those social relationships that I have managed to establish. I thrive in professional environments, and I have mastered the art of owning an audience in any professional setting. I am confident that I will fail you in social events, as I do not know how to navigate those settings. I communicate via text or email almost always. However, I promise that I am working diligently on changing this habit of mine.

You see, with all that I have experienced and learned as it pertains to love and relationships, I can guarantee you that you are acquiring a rare gem.

I am not in search of a perfect husband; I am already married to one. His name is Jesus. Instead, I desire and passionately long to attain oneness with you, whose life experiences have groomed you to be deserving of my love.

Through my life's journey, I have been prepared for your arrival. For this reason, I will embrace all of your imperfections. I recognize in advance that I will be sharing my precious life with another human being who, with all of his desires for greatness, will never amount to being perfect, and neither will I. And so, my darling, I promise to love you unconditionally with all your imperfections until death.

In life, one has to lead with set expectations, virtues, moral character, integrity, honesty, purity, loyalty, and the ability to seek right from wrong. I hope that through your life's journeys, God has gracefully bestowed these traits upon you, as I highly value them all. If not, I ask that you earnestly pray for God's divine favor in attaining these qualities, because they have helped define the woman who is going to be your wife. These values and traits are my core principles that shape my daily life. I can assure you that with these principles, we will never lack the prosperity and zeal needed to withstand the test of being imperfect human beings.

For most of my adult life, I have been told to tame these principles and minimize my expectations, as they are considered excessive. I will trust that, in due time, God will weed out what He deems unnecessary. My beloved, have no fear of the woman who is going to be your wife. As Solomon stated in Proverbs 18:22 (ESV), "He who finds a wife finds a good thing and obtains favor from the Lord." Well, darling, you sure have found a good thing and have obtained favor from the Lord!

Becoming one implies that we will be establishing an unbreakable bond. Therefore, when life beats us to the core and we are challenged by hardships, you will always have a shoulder to lean on in me, as I already know that I will have your shoulder to lean on, too. If or when you fail at any of your undertakings, I will be your greatest supporter, as you will be mine.

If or when you are put to the test, as I know you will be, because there are many beautiful women out there, I hope that you will remember the vow you took, the unity we have established, and most importantly, that you would be delivering one of the greatest pains that I may experience should you allow temptation to override our unity. I would like you to remember that you are valued and loved unconditionally. Hence, should you not fight off temptation, it will be devastating to our union. I can assure you that I will be eternally faithful to you, because I am confident that I am marrying the love of my life and your love will be sufficient.

When your friends invite you to "hang out" in places you know will bring temptations, please know that you are still an individual, and thus can make your own decisions. But, please understand that I will not tolerate infidelity. You can always count on me to be faithful to our union.

When we have a disagreement, I hope that we will be able to resolve our issues respectfully before going to bed without insults or cruel words toward one another.

When challenges arise, I hope that we will persevere and fight to the end for greatness.

I hope that we will hold fast to the truth that we will not be able to do anything without God's grace, love, and protection. I hope that you, too, believe in God and hold Him in high esteem, as He is going to be the foundational glue that holds our union together.

Being your wife will give me the desire to be the only woman whose affection and intimacy inspires you to reach your fullest potential. I hope that protecting my heart will be a constant desire of yours while endeavoring to protect the woman you have chosen to marry.

As we grow old and have navigated the storms in our relationship, I pray that I would still be the only woman who makes your heart beat faster than any race car or airplane out there, because you will be the only man who does it for me.

As it pertains to intimacy, I believe it is a treasured encounter that should be shared with mutual respect for one another. I desire for you to understand this.

I hope that you understand the value of teamwork, because being married will require us to work as a team. What's yours will become mine, and vice versa. Therefore, we should always share our opinions and communicate respectfully with one another.

I will count on you to love and respect my daughter and set great examples for her. I pray that you will never be tempted to violate or abuse her in any way. I desire that you gradually build a profound relationship with her that will help shape her for greatness, but most importantly, that you will come to love her as your own. You can count on me to do the same with your child or children, if you are already a parent.

I am an independent woman. I have navigated the roads of my life's journey alone, for the most part, but God's divine grace has directed my paths. However, just because I am independent does not mean that I will not need you to assume your role as the head of the household. As a team, I hope that we will strive to ensure financial stability for our family. Although I am perfectly capable of doing it all on my own, I still anticipate your arrival so I can hand you those roles that are meant for you. Even so, we will still be one in all.

If you are reading this letter and find yourself wanting to accept this invitation of becoming my future husband, I beg that you reassess your decision and deeply examine your motives. Should you find any discrepancies or doubts, please pass on me. If you are sorting yourself out from a previous heartbreak or are perhaps unraveling your position in your last union, please ignore me, as I am not a candidate for rebound, nor am I an experimental phase in which you can find your truth. I am not a candidate for a man who isn't ready to assume one of the most significant roles God has called him to assume, because He has diligently pruned me for your arrival. It only fits that we both are on the same page. I am writing this paragraph because it is just in my human nature to cover all bases. But, I am sure without any reservation that God will polish and refine you before sending you my way.

Psalm 127:1 (NIV) reads, "Unless the Lord builds the house, the builders labor in vain," which in essence implies that while we will be building a life together, if God is not present, then our efforts will be futile.

This letter stemmed from my conversations with Him about you! There's more, but these are my basic desires of my future husband that I know will solidify our union throughout eternity.

In anticipation of you,
Your future wife, Laura

Chapter Ten

Appeal to Love

"Laura, you have an intuitive mind." He continued, "It is unique, expandable, adjustable, and it adapts to everything."

I am quoting my former eighty-three-year-old client whom has since passed away. He did not know me well, but formed quite an impression of me. I was not sure what he meant by an "intuitive mind." Curious, I Googled the definition of the word "intuitive." Oh, goodness! It is such a huge compliment. I am not sure how he arrived at this conclusion, considering he only knew me for a short while, but I am honored he did, nevertheless.

While working with my former client one day, I shared with him a letter that I had written. After he read the letter, he suggested that I write about the fundamental principles that inspired me to write the letter, and that I also should write about what love means to me.

This particular letter, which I have titled "Dear Future Husband" in this book, was inspired by my lamentation to God about the pain I have endured thus far as it relates to love and relationships. "Appeal to Love" is inspired by courage—courage to reach deep within myself and express the underlying feelings that have always been at the core of my soul.

Are you ready for the journey?

Love, a four-letter word, has been in existence since the beginning of the world. I have heard it said that the word "love" is mentioned 761 times between the Old and New Testaments. Genesis 29:20 (NIV) reads, "So Jacob served seven years to get Rachel, but they seemed like only a few days to him because of his love for her."

At one time or another, everyone has experienced this divine emotion. Of course, the experience itself is unique. Although it is uniquely defined and expressed individually, love's profound depth of sensation is always to seek the same results from everyone. Love's secret desire is to manifest itself in the heart of the person experiencing it. Love's constant aim is to initiate, cultivate, nurture, and finally resonate while seeking to impress solely on its unique interpretation of self.

As a young girl, I always knew that my interpretation of love differed from many other people's. Although I must admit that thus far I have failed in my attempts to preserve love in my intimate relationships, these failures did not come as a result of my or my partners' deficiencies. Instead, my Heavenly Father has been sculpting me for His chosen son, with whom I will be matched to share His divine love, which can only be expressed in truth.

I cannot say that I have ever asked myself the definition of love, perhaps because I have known deep within that there's an explicit connection between love's nature and the soul of the person experiencing it. This truth about love has been validated with the relationships I have had and the experiences gained through these relationships. To me, love has never been a superficial emotion, because I have recognized from the start that the emotions felt were beautiful. When the pain and disappointments came, I knew these experiences were meant to shape my confidence in my journey to attain true love. I am seeking the kind of love that is not superficial, but that is designed by God's infinite grace.

To me, love is doing. Love is taught and not caught. However, love is often expressed as a misrepresentation of lust, and most often the desire to be in an intimate space with another person serves as a motivating factor that channels the passion of lust. In loving, however, there is a communicator and a receiver. Without one or the other, there's no love.

Love is universal. Love is colorblind. Love has no enemy and sees no faults. Love seeks to unite. Love endeavors where there are trials. Love's intimate triumph is when its confidence illuminates our darkest moments. Love is honesty. I have not found where honesty prevails, but darkness excels. Love is respect. Love infers that I value you. Love is courage. Love implies that we ought to persevere through the dark and clumsy times. Love is Providence, which is the validation that without God, love seeks not to exist.

What a profound sensation!

In reality, challenging ourselves to foster the desire to love and be loved requires grit and optimism. The truth is, love in itself is pure, flexible, but above all, love is hope. What do I mean by love is hope? The very foundation of love is hope. In my opinion, no one ever seeks love without first anticipating that his or her partner would dare to have the audacity of hope—hoping that the relationship would manifest into what each person desires and hopes to attain while becoming one, because hope is the perfect match through which love can be accessed.

It's clear that I have previously failed in my pursuit of true love. Be that as it may, my failures have not deterred me in my quest to attain this selfless and implicit love that is individually felt, but shared collectively. I know without a shadow of a doubt that my desire to attain true love will one day materialize. I am ready to experience love as I have never experienced it. Therefore, I am seeking the kind of love that inspires to find perfection, even though it will never succeed in attaining this goal due to our human nature. But, even then, I will be perfectly all right, because love always overcomes adversity and is resilient to failure.

Appeal to love.

About the Author

Laura Jaka has worked in social services for over two decades in various capacities, primarily in elderly care. In 2014 she established her private home-care company, Wellington Place of Serenity, which provides home-care services to both adults and children. Laura also works as a real estate agent.

Laura has one daughter, Camilla. She enjoys being a mom.

Laura's passion in life is to serve. She believes in making a difference in the lives of others, and diligently seeks to make an impact on the lives of those in need of support. Honoring this call to serve, Laura has pledged that a substantial part of the proceeds from the sale of this book will be donated to her nonprofit organization GRACE FOR MILE 6, which strives to provide assistance to the Mile 6 campsite where mudslide and flood victims in Sierra Leone currently reside. Laura's ultimate goal is to bring clean water, appropriate housing, and other primary necessities to Mile 6.

Laura believes that without the grace of God's mercy, which is the key foundational aspect of how she has been able to journey through life, her life would not be what it is today.

www.ingramcontent.com/pod-product-compliance
Lightning Source LLC
Chambersburg PA
CBHW060529080526
44586CB00012B/677